THE PRIVATE ADOLF LOOS

The Private Adolf Loos

Claire Beck Loos

Translated by
Constance C. Pontasch
Nicholas Saunders

Carrie Paterson *Editor*

DoppelHouse Press | Los Angeles

The Private Adolf Loos: Portrait of an Eccentric Genius
By Claire Beck Loos
Translated by Constance C. Pontasch and Nicholas Saunders
Edited by Carrie Paterson
© DoppelHouse Press, 2020 All rights reserved.

Adolf Loos Privat by Claire Beck Loos
Johannes-Presse, Vienna, Austria
© 1936 Claire Beck Loos

Book design: Carrie Paterson
Cover design: Carrie Paterson and Janet Lê

Publisher's Cataloging-in-Publication data
Names: Loos, Claire, author. | Pontasch, Constance C., translator. | Saunders, Nicholas, translator. | Paterson, Carrie, 1972-, editor.
Title: The Private Adolf Loos : portrait of an eccentric genius / by Claire Beck Loos ; translated by Constance C. Pontasch and Nicholas Saunders ; Carrie Paterson, editor.
Description: Los Angeles, CA : DoppelHouse Press, 2020.
Identifiers: LCCN: 2020931079 | ISBN: 9780997003482 | 9781733957939 (ebook)
Subjects: LCSH Loos, Adolf, 1870-1933. | Loos, Claire. | Architects--Austria--Biography. | Architects--Czechoslovakia--Biography. | Architects--Europe--Biography. | Architecture--Austria--Vienna--History--20th century. | Architecture--Czech republic--History--20th century. | Vila Müller (Prague, Czech Republic) | Jewish authors--Biography. | Jewish women--Biography. | Photographers--Czechoslovakia--Biography. | BISAC BIOGRAPHY & AUTOBIOGRAPHY / Artists, Architects, Photographers | BIOGRAPHY & AUTOBIOGRAPHY / Historical
Classification: LCC NA1038.L6 L62 2020 | DDC 720/.92/4--dc23
Printed in Canada

DoppelHouse Press | Los Angeles, California

Dedicated to Charles Paterson
in memorium

CONTENTS

REFLECTIONS OF A FEMALE PROTÉGÉ

An inscription by the author on a found second-hand copy of her 1936 book, *Adolf Loos Privat* [The Private Adolf Loos], is revealing: "In memory of a feverish time. Claire Beck Loos."

What follows is Claire's documentation of this passionate moment in culture, as well as her short-lived but impactful marriage to one of the great minds of the early-twentieth century. Through a penetrating view of her ex-husband, the architect Adolf Loos, she offers a dramatic and personal understanding of what it is to have spent time with a genius, an older mentor, and retain some of the creative psychic residue impressed by that experience.

Claire comes away from her time with Loos a changed person, and like anyone who has thrown himself or herself with abandon into a new mode of thinking — in rebellion or out of necessity — her struggle to integrate this moment into her life requires a generative act: this book. Through the unique form of her writing we learn not only about Loos and his work, but also about the role of emotional connections in forging new times.

CARRIE PATERSON, EDITOR

Adolf Loos in the living room of his apartment in Vienna, Giselastrasse 3,
now Bösendorferstraße, Vienna I, 1929.
Courtesy Janet Beck Wilson

PHOTO CLAIRE BECK

ADOLF LOOS
A SHORT BIOGRAPHY

Adolf Loos (December 10, 1870 – August 23, 1933) was born in Brunn (Brno, Czech Republic), the Moravian edge of Austro-Hungary. Son of a stonemason and sculptor, Loos studied architecture in Dresden from 1890–1893. He lived in the United States for three years following his education and then moved to Vienna to practice architecture in 1896. Within Vienna's lively fin-de-siècle café culture he began to formulate ideas on cultural reform and urban development, beginning what was virtually a second career as a writer and lecturer. He published articles in *Die Zeit*, *Die Wage*, and the *Neue Freie Presse*, but also briefly put out his own publication, *Das Andere* [The Other], which was a journal promoting "the introduction of Western Civilization into Austria." Loos' writings were later collected in several volumes, including *Ins Leere Gesprochen* [Spoken into the Void] in 1921, and *Trotzdem* [Nevertheless] in 1931; a portion have been translated into English as *Ornament and Crime, Selected Essays* (Ariadne Press, 1998), some of which are reprinted at the end of this volume.

In addition to his written work, Loos gave some sixty lectures from 1910 onward to audiences in Vienna, Prague, Brno, Berlin, Paris, Graz, and Munich.

Loos was influenced both by the Greek architect Vetruvius and Anglophone culture, and he incorporated aspects of classical architecture into his early work. Of these, a notable design was for the Chicago Tribune Tower (1922, unbuilt), a skyscraper in the form of a Greek column. Loos' use of iconography was short-lived, as he turned his attention to revolutionizing building practices, valorizing the craftsman and the laborer, opposing the "wasteful" ornamentation of the Viennese Secession and objecting loudly to mixing art and craft (epitomized by the work of his archenemies Koloman Moser and Josef Hoffmann at the Wiener Werkstätte), as well as pioneering the use of raw materials for their simplicity and beauty.

Loos' most radical project in Vienna, his Goldman & Salatsch building (1909–1911) on the Michaelerplatz, became colloquially known as "the building without eyebrows." Its defining distinction is a complete lack of ornamentation on the facade, which reputedly so offended Emperor Franz Josef that he refused to exit the Hofburg Palace on the side facing the "Loos Haus." Among Vienna's other Loosian attractions are the Café Museum (1899), The American Bar (or Kärntnerbar, 1907), Kniže Men's Outfitters (1909–1913) and his contribution to the Werkbundsiedlung housing project, a duplex (1931–1932).

During his lifetime Loos designed, built, and remodeled close to one hundred apartments and homes, and undertook a number of large civic projects like schools, government buildings, and workers' housing. Dozens of additional works included sanatoriums, hotels, cafés and bars, and shops. Several of Loos' projects were not realized but still remain influential, like the black-and-white striped marble house for Josephine Baker (1928) with its dramatic lighting and view underwater into the swimming pool.

Most relevant to this book, with its domestic and intimate qualities, are Loos' striking interiors. Using marble and wood veneers, beautiful hardwoods, brightly colored paints, glass block, mirror, photo murals, and even fur (for the bedroom of his first wife, Lina Loos), he transformed and sensualized the experience of space. His revolutionary open floor plans and stepped half-floors, sometimes conceived in a café and drawn on a napkin, created cubic arrangements; this intuitive method, coined the *Raumplan* by one of his students, came to full expression during the time period of Claire's narrative. Considered one of his most important contributions to Modern architecture, the Villa Müller (1928–30) in Prague, now a museum, is an excellent example of his highly evolved architectural philosophy.

But his work was neither immediately accepted nor appreciated, and Loos expressed constantly his feeling that he was either ignored or not properly recognized. As noted architecture historian Otto Kapfinger writes in his Afterword to the 2007 German edition of *Adolf Loos Privat*,

Loos was one of the most important reformers, innovators, and architectural critics of the 20th century. Internationally, the amount of literature written about his life's work has increased tremendously in recent decades. During the course of his lifetime, Loos' efforts in the area of architectural and practical design for everyday application through which he strove "to free humanity from superfluous labor" generally garnered him more ridicule and misunderstanding than anything else. Only a very few, like-minded people were able, or even wanted to accept this cultural reformer — an extremely exacting "destroyer of clutter," where ideals and materials were concerned.

Texts contemporaneous to Loos' era reinforce these ideas; take, for exmaple, critic Alfred Polgar's partly tongue-in-cheek defense of Loos' character in *Das Tagebuch* on September 13, 1928:

Loos has a lot to answer for. [...] He is an obstinate man who has frequently and vehemently objected to Viennese taste in matters of art and lifestyle and who has not only expressed totally unique, revolutionary views, but insisted he is right in every respect. He has revered and advocated the philosophy of Peter Altenberg and other revolting people. [...] He obliged Kokoschka to become a genius by bringing him to attention of the public early on. He championed acceptance of the most modern music as legitimate — a position which could be chalked up to his hearing loss — when it was still contended that it might not rightfully be considered music at all. Undoubtedly an additional side effect of his deafness, Loos states his opinion very loudly — in the metaphorical sense loudly. He forces one to listen. Contemporary cultural history, regardless of which position it may take or what evaluation it may make, will have to devote a long page to his unrelenting, passionate, fierce battle against ornamentation, against the mishmash of art and craft. In regard to aesthetic beliefs, he is fanatical to the point of being so just to be difficult; one could say, orthoparadoxical. He is a master of formulation, an absolute stylist, as caustic and witty in his attacks as he is in defense. In short, he is a man of eccentricities, of merit, of importance.

These contradictions were lost neither on his enemies nor his friends. For his sixtieth birthday Stefan Zweig wrote,

> Explosive in his words and at the same time productive in his works, [Loos] demonstrates in his creations just as much prudent, far-sighted, moderate harmony as in his spirit an energetic and passionate revolt — that splendid unity of blood and spirit that only creates life and liveliness!

Indeed, it is the heterogeneity of his expression in both word and form that continue to fascinate, frustrate, and intrigue.

In the years since his death, Loos has been canonized in architecture, become the subject of many books, and retrospective exhibitions have taken place in locales around the world; among these: Berlin (1984–1985), Vienna (1989–1990, 2014, and others), Prague (2010, 2019, and 2020), Brno (2010), London (2011), Pilsen (2012), New York (1985 and 2013), Barcelona (2017–2018), with more undoubtedly to come. Among his peers, he garnered great respect — an architect's architect, who ultimately stood for dignity and parity, and for the people.

Le Corbusier's assessment of this unlikely hero: "Loos swept right beneath our feet, and it was a Homeric cleansing — precise, philosophical and logical. In this, Loos has had a decisive influence on the destiny of architecture."[*]

---

* *Frankfurter Allgemeine Zeitung*, 1930; quoted in Rukschcio, Burkhardt and Roland Schachel, *Adolf Loos: Leben und Werk* (Vienna: Residenz Verlag, 1982) 278.

Claire Beck Loos, circa late 1930s.
Possible self-portrait.

CLAIRE BECK LOOS
THE FRACTURED LENS

Claire (Klara) Beck Loos (November 4, 1904 – January 15,* 1942) was an author and photographer, born to an affluent Jewish family of industrialists in Pilsen (Plzeň, Czech Republic), in what was then the Hapsburg Empire. She became the third wife of Adolf Loos in 1929 and three years after his death, memorialized him in this book intended to raise money for Loos' tombstone.

Claire Beck was trained in photography and worked professionally in the atelier of Hede Pollak in Prague. For her formal studies, she had attended the *Graphische Lehr- und Versuchsanstalt*, an art school in Vienna with a well-respected photography program. She seems to have experimented with self-portraiture, as several of her surviving photographs show.

Though Claire took many images of Loos herself, she chose to use Pollak's famous portrait of him on her book cover. This English language edition features many of Claire's own portraits of Loos, including her most famous: Loos standing in front of his fireplace in Vienna with his ear horn, which for years has hung outside the preserved rooms of his Giselastraße apartment that are now installed at the Wien Museum.

---

* Date of death unknown. Given is the departure date of Claire's four-day transport, number P-785, from Theresienstadt (Terezín) to the Nazi extermination camp in Riga, Latvia (Gottwaldt, Alfred and Diana Schulle. *Die "Judendeportationen" aus dem Deutschen Reich 1941–1945* [Wiesbaden: Marix Verlag, 2005] 132).

Claire and Loos divorced in 1932, more about which is discussed in the following pages. After that, she lived an itinerant artist's life. Documents indicate she stayed at various times in Pilsen, Prague, and Vienna; shortly after Nazi stamps appear in her passport, when she traveled to Vienna in August 1938, (at roughly the same time that her sister's family fled to the Becks' in Pilsen), it appears she got a Bulgarian transit visa.

During the two difficult years she spent in Prague between 1940 and 1941, living under Nazi occupation, she had a job as an unpaid assistant for another photographer. This fact is known through letters from Claire and her mother Olga Beck, which have been preserved since the war years by Claire's surviving family. That photographer was making images in the style of the Bewegung, an art movement that had influenced Loos, and to which Claire had most likely been exposed during a time of artistic experimentation in Paris. After Loos died, Claire continued her associations with his friend Max Thun-Hohenstein, a movement researcher attached to the Bewegung; a surviving photograph of her sister Eva suggests Claire had also been interested in photographing modern dancers. By working for this unnamed photographer, we know that Claire was experimenting with a Leica camera. She did this among other odd jobs she could find, including being a baker's assistant.

Outside of what has been preserved by her surviving family and by Loos collectors, little of Claire's photographic record is known to remain. Her letters suggest she actively pursued her vocation until she was caught up in Nazi deportations and the

Holocaust. She writes that the landlord of one of her apartments in Prague allowed her to set up a darkroom, a generous act, as she would have been very limited in her abilities to go out in public by curfews and the imposition of wearing the Jewish Star of David, much less having means to purchase necessary supplies. Claire's last photographs from this period, and indeed any other photos she may have been taken of Loos and his circle, are lost, as much of the contents of her safety deposit box at the Escompte- und Creditbank in Prague that she opened in 1939 was looted as Jewish property after the Nazi invasion of Czechoslovakia.

One can only wonder what Claire kept of letters or mementos, and equally importantly, what her artistic output was or could have been had she lived beyond the war. Her memories and photographs that have survived her, meanwhile, continue to tell the story of Adolf Loos, her primary known subject outside of her family. For years, her anecdotes about Loos could be found peppering others' texts but without attribution, and her photographs were used sometimes without credit. This began to change when Burkhardt Rukschcio met Claire's brother Max Beck in England and included information about her in his authoritative monograph with Roland Schachel *Adolf Loos: Leben und Werk* (Vienna: Residenz Verlag, 1982) and again when editor and filmmaker Adolf Opel republished *Adolf Loos Privat* in German in 1985 with informative supplemental materials, including photographs and testimony from Max Beck given informally at a conference on Loos at the

Warburg Institute.

Translations of *Adolf Loos Privat* have now appeared in English (2011), Czech (2013), and Italian (2014) and a work of historical fiction closely based on Claire's life, *Le Scarpe di Klara* [Klara's Shoes] by Wolftraude di Concini appeared in Italian in 2018 (Publistampa Edizioni). In 2012–2013, Claire's photographs were included alongside her much more famous contemporaries like Trude Fleischmann and Madame d'Ora in an exhibition at the Jewish Museum entitled *Vienna's Shooting Girls: Jewish Women Photographers in Vienna*, curated by Iris Meder. And starting in 2017, the West Bohemian Writers' Association has presented exhibitions and literary symposia about Claire Beck Loos and her book at several locales in Pilsen. The exhibition has also traveled to Brno, Brussels, and Riga, with Liberec and other cities still planned. Since 2012, the organizer, David Růžička, has given public presentations, readings, and written several articles about Claire which have appeared in magazines with circulations of up to 100,000 in the Czech Republic, turning her into a minor local celebrity and inspiring artwork, radio readings, television features, and further research into her life.

In these ways, Claire Beck Loos' observations of her husband have now — approaching one hundred years later — returned the gaze fittingly back toward her.

INTRODUCTION TO
THE PRIVATE ADOLF LOOS

Adolf Loos Privat was first published in 1936, three years after Loos died. Since its publication, this short biography has been hailed as a small jewel of literature composed of snapshot-like vignettes, a portrait of a man and mentor as seen by his young wife and caretaker, interpreter, secretary, and often proxy.

Loos had suffered long-standing health complications, which rendered him ultimately mute and deaf. During Loos' particularly serious bout of illness in 1931, Claire recorded his wishes for tombstone. A year after his death, he was conferred a "grave of honor" when his body was moved to the Zentralfriedhof in Vienna to rest amongst the city's finest writers, composers, and cultural icons; but it was not until 1956, however, that the grey granite block he had specified would be installed. Claire seems to have imagined this short book to become a memorial in its own right, especially as the architectural monument he had desired did not seem to be forthcoming.

Correspondence from the 1930s between Claire and the Loos expert and collector Dr. Ludwig Münz document the lengths to which the Beck family went in order to raise funds for Loos' self-specified grave marker (cf. letter between Münz and Max Beck, page 218). When funds from initial book sales were not enough, Claire also solicited Loos' friends and admirers for the remaining balance, calling on those like Loos' former student Kurt Unger (as Claire once wrote, "Loos' warrior"), who had provided for Loos financially toward the end of his life, and possibly notable figures like Czechoslovakia's national poet, Josef Svatopluk Machar, as well as the country's first president, Tomáš Garrigue Masaryk (cf. letter between Claire and Machar, page 219). How successful she was in this endeavor is still unclear.

At Loos' gravesite on August 25, 1933 — where Claire's passport details suggest that she was in attendance — Karl Kraus, Loos' friend and comrade-in-arms as a cultural reformer, addressed his departed friend in his eulogy:

> You were forever committed to the future. [...] Your genius, through the removal of ornate obstacles to beauty, emancipated life from bondage to the commonplace, and diverted it from the circuitous. [...] You have garnered — as does every person who leaves a legacy to future generations — considerable ingratitude from those living all too much in the present: a resistance which stems from the nebulous perception that a larger-than-life figure has emerged — one who will outlive them — a disruptor of disorder.

As with so many of Loos' friends, Kraus held deep admiration for the man, which continues to translate through generations.

Through Claire it is possible to hear the words of this Loos, a more intimate account than the one recorded by experts and historians. To this point, Adolf Opel writes in *Adolf Loos — Der Mensch* [Adolf Loos — The Man],

> [Claire's] portrait of Loos is completely uncritical, and she omits almost entirely any exact dates and facts regarding Adolf Loos'

work. Still, her book exudes an air of authenticity, no doubt due to the fact that such a short period of time had passed between the recounted events and her recording of them. By the end of 1935, Claire Loos had already published short excerpts from her book in [two Viennese newspapers,] the *Neue Freie Presse* and *Wiener Tag*. *Adolf Loos Privat* appeared following them in early 1936, published by Johannes-Presse in Vienna — a publisher affiliated with the Neue Galerie of Otto Nirenstein (Kallir), [who was] a Schiele collector.

During Claire and Loos' time together she heard his affection, his scorn, his aphorisms and stories, and transcribed his dictations, which bordered on histrionics when he was ill. With his manner of speaking quite clearly ingrained, Claire leaves the reader with a sense of living with the man, and makes it possible to hear some semblance of the way Loos talked — to friends, clients, wives, students, craftsmen, artists, and society.

But one can also read in Claire Beck Loos' work a mirroring of the last collection of Loos' writings, *Trotzdem*, published in 1931; her similar spare style is what so vividly reenacts his personality, creating a bricolage of images, narrative, and dialogue. While her memory of him is flattering at times, it is not at others. But regardless, hers is a welcome and humanizing counter-balance to the reification of "the great God Loos" as he was called by his admirers and friends in his lifetime and postmortem. When the *Neue Freie Presse* published excerpts on the second anniversary of Loos' death, the newspaper praised *Adolf Loos Privat* as "valuable" and "a document humain," and a positive review was published by composer Ernst Krenek.

Readers of this book today will need to keep in mind that Claire's retrospective memoir captures not only the personal and social transformative power of Loos' work, but also figures the contradictions of the man as a sign of the times. On July 4, 1929, Loos wrote to Claire that he liked the Jews "better than people from Vienna," barely a compliment. Separately, with some irony, he called himself an "anti-Semite" and made no secret of having had several Jewish wives. A short chapter reveals Claire's emphasis on such statements and lays bare Loos' internal logic, which was convoluted and perhaps reactionary, but which at the same time places him within larger trends toward anti-Semitism in public discourse that was already apparent in the 1930s.

Claire shows these insidious effects in certain discomfiting instances by flipping between the first and third person, as if she is both inhabiting the frame, but at the same time watching herself like a character in it. This dissociative process may reflect her outsider status, a feeling of abjectness both privately as a woman and in the larger social narrative as a Jew (though she had been baptised when she was a child, presumably to remove stigma). Yet a love story it is, and no matter how abject she feels, she portrays herself always redeemed in the eyes of her husband, Adolf Loos.

While Claire and Loos' marriage lasted only a few years, she lived nearly her whole life under the unifying coherence of his architecture. As Opel describes more fully in *Adolf Loos — Der Mensch*, informed by interviews with Claire's brother Max Beck,

An association between Claire's [parents], Otto [and Olga Feigl] Beck — who had made [their] fortune in the iron [wire] and commercial hops industries — and Adolf Loos began prior to World War I. In 1907, Otto Beck had commissioned Loos to furnish his apartment in Pilsen. In 1928, Loos relocated the apartment to a different site in Pilsen to which the Beck family had moved. It was during this period that the almost 60-year-old Loos decided to marry the 24-year-old Claire Beck. She, a professional photographer, had already developed — along with her artistic vocation — a Bohemian penchant for independence, a lifestyle she chose in defiance of her family and eschewing the brewery city of Pilsen. She departed for Paris, where she hoped to join its Bohemian culture. It was there that she also became reacquainted with Adolf Loos, who had taken up residence in Paris in the late 1920s, and who was struggling to procure commissions. Claire's parents were against a marriage of the two for several reasons, not the least of which was the age difference of 34 years. Moreover, there had been a colossal scandal involving Loos in 1928 — a case involving moral impropriety, which was mercilessly exploited by the tabloids. Allegations made against him by three minor girls led to a trial and sentencing with probation.

The "scandal" related here has been discussed in other publications, including Christopher Long's dramatic and well researched account, *Adolf Loos on Trial* (Kant, 2017), which shows how the proceedings became in some ways a referendum on the avant-garde and its perceived immorality. Claire has little to say about this episode, but she does comment, with some sarcasm, on

Loos' humane response to prostitutes: that he and his close friend, Oskar Kokoschka would try to "*save*" them (author's emphasis); that Loos would invite them to his house for lunch or parties along with anyone: carpenters, clients, the demimonde, students, etc.; and that Loos was, if anything, an idealist and great social equalizer.

Claire didn't have an easy marriage to Loos, though by all accounts, including her own, she knew what she was getting into. They married on July 18, 1929. As Opel tells it,

> Before the year was out, Loos became extremely ill and had to be transported to the Cottage Sanatorium in serious condition. In the following two years — and thus for the entire duration of this short marriage — Adolf Loos repeatedly required treatment at health resorts and sanatoriums. Aside from the two focal points of Pilsen and Prague, where he completed his last projects, one finds traces of Adolf Loos during these years in Karlsbad and Baden near Vienna. The Loos [couple] also returned frequently to Vienna, where the pair stayed in hotels and boardinghouses as Loos had become too frail to climb the stairs to his sixth-story apartment. In addition, he had been forced to sublet his apartment on several occasions in order to keep up with pressing debts.

In 1931, between March and July, Loos and Claire traveled through Germany, Switzerland, and Italy on their way to the Riviera, before heading back to Paris. They stopped on their way through, or stayed at, Nürnberg, Frankfurt, Mannheim, Heidelberg, Darmstadt, Stuttgart, Zürich, Milan, Nice, Cap d'Antibes, Juan les Pins, Cannes, and on their way to Paris, went through the mountains between the Riviera and Lyon. They arrived in Paris at the Café du Dôme, which had been known since the turn of the century as a gathering place for intellectuals and artists.

It was a fantastic voyage, but it was doomed. Loos and Claire separated in Paris, in 1931. A brief missive Loos wrote to his student Kurt Unger on October 29, 1931, contains rumors of Claire being romantically involved with others, one named simply as "Bauer." By January 1932 Claire had requested formal divorce papers through a client of Loos in Vienna, the lawyer Dr. Gustav Scheu. After this, Claire may have attended another art school; but she never remarried, and she kept "Loos" as her last name.

As for the fates of the Beck family, Claire's father Otto Beck died in 1934 and was buried in Pilsen. Claire and her mother, Olga, remained in Czechoslovakia through the Nazi invasion and had every intention to emigrate to join their surviving family in England or New York. However, in the end they could not obtain visas — neither to Cuba nor Ecuador, the two last hopes they had before they were called up for deportation on Nazi-requisitioned trains to "the East." In one of her last letters, she writes about trying to send her books out of Europe to her brother-in-law in New York — could those have been versions of the book you hold in your hand?

Through her photography and her book, and because of Loos, something of Claire survives. The traces of her work that we can see suggest there was more, that she accomplished more, but in the brevity of her life and manner of her death, this

27

remains only supposition about an unrealized potential.

What we do know is that *Adolf Loos Privat* distinguishes itself through its literary experimentation and use of language. Akin to a work of modern architecture, it uses an efficient, precise, and spare vocabulary, with little ornamentation. Unlike traditional German, often an unwieldy, clause-bloated language, Claire writes in short sentences and chooses words that are straightforward and which punctuate space with a consistent measure. It's as if she imagines having to parse her phrases to the nearly-deaf Loos. Perhaps her first vignette is even an indication for the reader of the approach one might take with the book — that it could be read out loud — and thus Claire's stories about Loos might be enjoyed much as his own writings were in the coffeehouses, in dialogue with other people.

Part performance, part memorial, Claire brings her own voice alive in concert and contraposto with Loos. Claire is referred to by Loos as "Klara," "Kläre," "Lerle," and "Lärle;" she called him "Dolf" and "Dolfi." Comedic timing relates Claire's sense of humor about the ludicrous situations in which she finds herself. The madcap adventures with Loos feel tangible. And no matter its strange or unlikely context, a love story at heart still it is.

Cues from Loos' letters fill out these impressions. Loos misses her "sweet saxophone voice" (April 8, 1929); when he proposes to her, the response is "a great poem in prose" (June 25, 1929). After he finishes a serial novel in the newspaper he imagines she could have written it (July 4, 1929). They agree to wed, and he sends her "thousands of kisses everywhere, your husband Dolf." Further elements from Loos' letters to Claire can be found in an appendix here. However, the content of what she expressed to him in her letters will remain for us unfortunately a mystery, as a fire destroyed many of the Loos papers.

At the end of Claire's book we are left with the distinct impression that even after their divorce, their love continued. She has elided certain details, nevertheless, which we learn about in the journal of Loos' builder in Pilsen from 1928 onward, Bořivoj Kriegerbeck (1891–1975). Namely, there is one episode right before the divorce of a jealous spat between Claire and Loos' nursemaid, Annie ("a Prague beauty"), who Loos expressed interest to marry in a letter to his right-hand man, Heinrich Kulka, despite being extremely ill at the end of his life. Kriegerbeck's journal reveals Annie's misimpression that Loos was "very rich." When Claire sees Annie with Loos at the sanatorium, according to Kriegerbeck, "They hurled themselves at each other and fought, pulling each other's hair. Loos, when he saw it, took his [walking] stick ... and attacked his former wife," trying to separate them. But then they all went to lunch as "an orderly family group," though no doubt Claire's ego suffered and, Kriegerbeck reports, her body was also bruised.

What we can tell is that nearly everyone who came into contact with Loos became fanatically attached to him, devoted each for their own reasons and to their own ends. This remains true of his legacy: and so, dear reader, once you know the man in your own private capacity, you too may find him unforgettable.

Adolf Loos privat

The original 1936 dust jacket for *Adolf Loos Privat* by Claire Beck Loos, with Loos portrait by Hede Pollak, Prague, and script in red.

An announcement for the book by the publisher states, "In this book, Mrs. Loos, the last wife of the great master who died much too early, tells about the last years of his life, and a great deal about his last works and the people who crossed his path during this time. The form of the story that Mrs. Loos chooses is very lively, and it contains snapshots of immediate freshness. For all his friends and admirers, this book will be a discovery and a reminiscence of this great time. The book will appear in the size of 12 x 17 cm and has roughly 160 pages."

The Private Adolf Loos

FOREWORD

I have written this book from memory. I have tried to portray Adolf Loos in a form that will hopefully give the reader an understanding of his strong personality. I am aware of the shortcomings that are inherent to this kind of reporting, but have nevertheless chosen to write this way, as it seemed important to me to preserve in the material the vitality that came from living together with Loos. Should errors in my recollections, which I can no longer verify today, have crept in then I ask that they be forgiven, considering what I have said above. Remaining plans, notes, drawings and letters will be compiled in other books by experts; my book should therefore not be viewed as a reference book but instead simply as a remembrance of my life with Adolf Loos.

I am dedicating the royalties from this book as a contribution towards establishing Loos' tomb.

CLAIRE LOOS.

HOW IT ALL CAME ABOUT

A stranger asks my father: "How did you make the acquaintance of Loos? How did you get to have Loos do your interior remodel?"

Father tells him: "I lived as a young man in a small provincial Austrian city. At the time, Adolf Loos' essays were being published in the *Neue Freie Presse*. I was only a very low ranking employee and did not have the money to subscribe to the newspaper. So I looked for it at the coffee house and read it there because I found Loos' articles very interesting. But a lot of people were in the same situation I was. There was always fighting over the newspaper and it was always gone. During one such dispute, a patron just decided to jump up on a table and began reading the article out loud.

"And that is what they did from then on. In those days the coffee house seemed to be more like a meeting place, and afterwards there would be a lot of discussion.

"It was my greatest desire to have Loos do my interior remodel someday... But it was many years until that would happen..."

THIS PICTURE HAS GOT TO GO

I am fifteen years old. I go into the big living room to get a book. Two men are there. One of them is Professor L., the other one I do not know. The stranger kneels halfway down onto the bench seat and removes a picture from the wall. He is wearing a brown suit and a cream-coloured shirt. His face is slender and youthful.

"I would just like to know," he says, "who painted this trash. This picture has got to go."

I say: "I painted this picture, and it was for my father's birthday!"

"Well, well," says the stranger, "for your father's birthday, that is of course another matter." Almost tenderly, he hangs the picture back up on the wall. "So you must be the daughter of the owner?"

"And you," I ask inquisitively, "who then are you?"

The stranger looks at me, smiling: "I am Adolf Loos!"

JOSEPHINE BAKER DANCES IN VIENNA

Josephine Baker is dancing in Vienna.

Loos, who has a business meeting with my father, invites all of us to the Varieté where Josephine Baker is dancing. Sitting beside the beautiful, intelligent Frau X. he looks eagerly at the stage and says: "Did you know that Josephine counts me among the best Charleston dancers in Paris?"

"That is certainly a compliment, dear Loos," says the beautiful woman, smiling.

"I have even earned money by dancing," Loos says proudly.

"Money by dancing?" Frau X. asks slowly, raising her eyebrows. "You really must tell us about that," she adds, amused.

Loos looks at Frau X. with an expression of pure, unadulterated joy. "It was quite simple: at an elegant bar, I asked a stranger to a dance. After the dance, she pressed a large coin into my hand."

"And you took the money?" asks Frau X., truly shocked.

Loos looks astonished at the dismayed expression on her face. "But of course. I have never been as proud of any money I earned as I was of that. Just think how well I must have danced and how wonderful I must have looked for her to have thought I was employed as a dancer there! But then, I had a perfect instructor: Josephine Baker! – – – Long live Josephine," Loos cries out loudly and applauds. Josephine appears, dressed in a few green feathers, and gracefully curtsies to all sides. "She did not recognize me," Loos says, hurt, "or else she definitely would have come over to our table."

Josephine dances. Loos watches her attentively. "I consider Josephine to be a very great artist," he says softly. "Just look at what grace and what strength there is in her movements. She always reminds me of an animal in the wild. But the people here have no understanding of her great art," he adds sadly. "They only see her beautiful body. In Paris it is quite different. There the whole house cheers with enthusiasm when Josephine dances." Loos falls silent. When Josephine finishes, he applauds with all his might, spurring the rest of the audience again and again to new roaring ovations.

Josephine now selects a partner from the audience. Amid general laughter, a good-natured elderly gentleman gets up on stage. "This number," Loos says, "was a huge success for Josephine in Prague. She had chosen a thin, agile man from the audience. It was none other than Vlasta Burian, the greatest Czech comedian. It would be impossible to describe her growing astonishment as Burian did the most amazing capers, for she was completely unaware who he was. The audience was screaming with laughter. But Josephine kept animating him to do new tricks." Loos laughs softly.

"Yes, Josephine is unique... Still, recently I did get upset with her. It was in Paris. She came to me and was in a bad mood. *Just think, Loos, she pouted, I want to do big, big remodelling in my house and do not like plans of architects.* I was beside myself. What, you did not come to me first? Don't you know that I can design the most beautiful plan in the world for you? Josephine stares at me with her childlike eyes and slowly asks: *You are an architect???* – She had no idea who I was. – I drew up a plan for Josephine... I consider it one of my best. The exterior wall is covered with white and black marble slabs – diagonally striped. The most beautiful thing in the house is the bathroom – with its ethereal lighting..." Just at that moment a red rose comes flying onto our table. Josephine has discovered Loos. With a graceful leap she is now at our table herself.

"Loos," she calls, "dear Loos, I so happy that you here," and with that she stretches out both hands to him. The great man blushes like a little boy.

After the performance, Loos says to me in a low voice so our companion cannot hear him: "Why don't you call me sometime? My number is in the telephone book. We could go out once by ourselves."

It seems incomprehensible to me that Loos can be
reached by telephone like any other mortal – – –

KÄRNTNERBAR

I meet Loos in front of the opera. We stroll along the Kärntnerstrasse. We stop in front of a bookstore and Loos draws my attention to a simple book cover that appeals to him. Right after that, he discovers in a display a cigarette case of light poplar. He decides to use poplar wood as paneling in a dining room in P. We turn into a side street and go into an elegant little bar. While we are sipping orangeade sitting on the high stools at the bar, Loos says: "I decorated this bar many years ago. It was the first American bar in Vienna. It was originally only thought of for men. The women were quite up in arms about that. Everyday it was packed and the bar overcrowded, but all women were turned away. Countesses and princesses would lead the way, they would beg and they would threaten, but it was no use. They were not allowed in. Public curiosity grew day by day. It was causing quite a sensation in all of Vienna and gave the bar a lot of free advertising. Finally, after five weeks, the situation became intolerable. The women forced their way in."

Loos points at the ceiling: "These marble panels caused a lot of trouble. The Italian specialist who had been working on them suddenly refused to put up the ceiling. He said: 'It will definitely fall down.' I answered: 'Put it up anyway.' The Italian became furious and threw himself at me. The very next minute he was ashamed of his conduct. He asked me for forgiveness and, filled with remorse, asked: 'How can I make up for this?' I answered calmly: 'Put up the ceiling.' It has to this day, after more than twenty years, not fallen down."

THINK IT OVER WELL

Loos is lying stretched out on a corner bench in the dining room asleep. Kulka, the architect, is sitting at the table with a worried look on his face. In front of him is a pile of letters and cards. He looks up for a moment as I come in, then points discontented to the mail. "Nothing but unanswered letters," he sighs. "And then the master is surprised when he loses projects." I sit down quietly at the table. "You know, in the past I always used to do that work," he continues, "but now I have my own business. There is not enough time. The poor master cannot do everything himself either. And then there are always people distracting him from his work." Kulka looks over to the sleeping man with a gently reproachful look. I immerse myself in thought, moved by his words. Kulka is right. Adolf Loos, the great man, gives away his heart, his strength to everybody who comes to him for help. But who helps him? And then, as if Kulka had read my thoughts, he says: "No one helps him. Everyone just comes to him for help. Couldn't you take care of a little of this abandoned mail? Adolf Loos needs someone."

"Do you think, Herr Kulka," I ask timidly, "that I can really help him?"

Kulka, the architect, looks at me with a friendly

expression: "Give it a try."

I sort the mail into a letter file, which Kulka has quickly supplied. Suddenly Loos awakens. He sits up, yawns, clears his throat, clears his throat more loudly as if to assure himself he isn't dreaming... There is a look of total astonishment on his face. Suddenly, he joyously exclaims: "Would you like to always stay with me and work with me? Until now, I have always worked for my women and have tried to make them great and famous, as actresses, dancers. What for? What for? Maybe they would've been happier to remain with me and darn socks."

Loos falls silent, gazes off into space. Suddenly, his face brightens. He stands up, takes both of my hands: "But you, you will become no actress, no dancer. You will work with me. It is not easy. Think it over well. My life is a chain of disappointments..."

LOOS HELPS OUT

I am invited to dine at Loos'. Besides me, there is another guest present, R. P., a young writer. Loos had not even known him before. A few things he read from him pleased him very much. He invited him. As the young artist describes to Loos his difficult situation – he has a family to support –, Loos is very touched. He promises to help. "In Vienna I can do little for you. Go to Berlin. I have good friends there, I will give you some recommendations." Without asking the young man any further, Loos buys him a ticket to Berlin.

A few weeks later a letter arrives from Berlin:

March 19, 1929

Dear Herr Loos!

Myself, my wife, and my child send you our sincere, and best regards. Things will start moving ahead here; it is just a little hard in the beginning with a family. Starting on April 1 however, I will have a steady job. I just have to hang on until then. I hope that you are in good health.

Your ever-thankful

R. P.

"Wait," says Loos, "with what?" So he calls up a wealthy client: "Please send some money to R. P. immediately."

ON THE LAURENZIBERG

We are in Prague. We are walking up the Laurenziberg. It is spring and everything is in bloom. Loos speaks:

"On top of the Laurenziberg I would like to build a hotel; it would fit in well with the landscape. A second Kobenzl... Just think, the Hradshin, this magnificent view and as its complement the Laurenziberg with a hotel that can be seen from far away! I have a plan in mind... a wonderful plan! The cable railway would have to be put back into operation again; visitors from all over the world would stay there. Something like that is missing in Prague!"

Chatting along like this, we have reached the top of the Laurenziberg. There is a little measly tavern. We order two glasses of curdled milk. The innkeeper, a fat woman with an unfriendly face, sets them in front of us without a word. Dusk is starting to fall.

"In the evening," Loos continues to fantasize, "when Prague is shining with the sparkle of lights, what a view the lucky residents of the hotel would enjoy!" Loos stares contemplatively into the distance. "Oh, Lerle, how happy I would be if I could build that hotel," he says humbly, "How nice would that be...!" Suddenly: "I left my wallet behind in the hotel. Do you have any money with you?" I have none. "I don't even have my watch with me."

We look at each other without word. Both of us are thinking of the mean face of the innkeeper. "Come on then," I murmur. Silently we take each other's hands... we will come back sometime soon and pay. Hand in hand, we walk down the mountain. The path seems endless. What will the innkeeper say when she finds the abandoned glasses we barely touched?!

SHIMMERING FISH

The construction of the Müller house is still in the very early stages. Dr. Müller has taken Loos to the construction site for a meeting. Loos stands between some beams and points to a location. "Here," he says, "is where the illuminated aquarium with the fish will be." No one understands him. The client wants to move on – there are so many important things to discuss. But Loos remains still, unconcerned, and continues: "This will be the favorite place of the master of the house; when he comes home in the evening tired from work, he will watch the fish silently playing. In the light of the lamps they will shimmer in all colours." The client is already getting very annoyed, but Loos does not let it bother him. He – the only one who does not see the boards and scaffolds but rather the finished house – talks today only of the shimmering fish.

SCHÖNBERG'S GURRELIEDER IS
PERFORMED IN VIENNA ...

Loos recounts: "I can remember the premiere performance as if it were yesterday! Not one ticket had been sold by noon. On the spur of the moment, I took the last of my money and bought up the entire concert hall. Then I stood on the Kärntnerstrasse and handed out tickets to acquaintances and strangers – whoever came my way. That evening the hall was packed full. Some friends and I had scattered ourselves throughout the entire concert hall so that we could intervene in the event of an uproar. My wife Bessie was in the gallery.

"Sure enough, hissing and grumbling did break out after the first movement. My wife threw herself like a beast at the disrupters and began walloping them... Yes, Bessie was quite a character!" Loos falls wistfully silent. (Bessie had died of pulmonary disease).

"Have you ever heard the *Gurrelieder*?" I answer no. "Oh, Lerle, what a shame, I know them by heart!" Losing himself in thought, he begins to hum to himself, then sings out, purely and clearly, a main motif. Suddenly he turns silent, his eyes open wide, contorting with fear. "Lerle, Lerle, do you hear me?" Thinking back, he has forgotten his deafness. "Lerle, I can't hear anymore, I am completely deaf!" He claps both hands in front of his face with a painful, lamenting cry; then, quietly straightening up, he begins to sing again – this time very loudly, with wide-opened eyes. I grab the ear horn and hand it to him. Hesitating, he puts it up to his ear and looks at me with questioning, anxious eyes. As loudly as I can, I repeat the motif into the ear horn.

"Not so loud, I am not deaf you know," he shouts delighted. A smile moves over his face, coming to rest in his golden brown eyes. "Sing it again, Lerle," he softly implores, "It sounds so beautiful!" I sing. "Now, repeat it! Have you memorized it?" I nod.

Now Loos begins to sing the next motif of the *Gurrelieder*. He explains all the voices to me, the entire structure, the content, we work on it all day long until evening falls...

JAN SLIVINSKI

One day Jan Slivinski-Effenberger arrives from Paris. With his warmth, his happy disposition, his intelligent mind, he fills the whole apartment, makes life beautiful again. He has brought along a large suitcase and does not ever want to leave. He awakens the old dusty piano out of its silence and coaxes the most wonderful melodies out of it.

Loos looks at him, smiling. He does not hear him, but he watches him, how he sits comfortably at the piano and searchingly reaches for the chords. He makes a fascinating impression, his handsome, intelligent head slightly tilted back. This is the beginning of a happy period. The evil of people and everything depressing is forgotten. Every day is a new celebration. Jan Slivinski has such a strong personality.

Loos says: "Slivinski is a person who cannot stay long in one occupation. He always needs something new. But he is no dilettante, he has always fully completed each occupation he was in. He always was a master! Years ago, he was in charge of the Kaiser's library. Later, he became a piano virtuoso and singer. He worked together with Tagore to translate his poems from English into German. In Paris, he owned a large bookstore. Before that, he fought for the freedom of Poland. But his dream was to become a great singer. His voice was magnificent... He almost lost it during the war... That was his most painful ordeal..."

Slivinski has become much more than a great singer... He is a whole person! Everyone who came to him, he has helped... He has discovered many artists... He went with Loos and Kokoschka into the small bars of Paris and tried to "save" poor young girls.

Also in Vienna, we went on pilgrimages together to the nightclubs. We usually ended our expeditions at the Reiss Bar. This is where the artists of Vienna congregate. All of them simply drop in there whenever they feel like it. Loos particularly enjoyed it when Hollitzer, who had such a unique personality, and was as powerful and impressive as a mighty tree, would sing...

LOOS AT WORK

The daily routine for Loos is as follows: In the morning at eight-thirty, Wipsi, the dog, is let into the room. He is a gentle alarm clock. Then Mitzi comes in with breakfast. This consists of a cup of coffee and two croissants with butter and honey. About this time, Suchanek – the carpenter – or the wall-paperer will often come to discuss some project with Loos. Other visitors are not allowed in, they have to wait in the dining room until Loos has bathed and dressed. The conversation with the workers, however, will often be carried on through the bathroom door.

Around eleven-thirty Loos takes a short walk. He strolls along the Kärntnerstrasse.

The highlight of the day is lunch at twelve-thirty. There are guests every day. Here, one can meet people from all over the world. Artists, scholars and those who would like to become them, clients, schoolboys, students, female dancers, grand ladies, demi-monde women. Loos knows how to bridge the gap between the most extreme opposites of an often motley assembly. He will often bring a guest with him even at the last moment.

After some black coffee, Loos rests for at least half an hour unconcerned whether or not guests are still there. Sometimes the guests simply stay seated at the table and continue chatting with one another. They do not bother him; he certainly cannot hear them.

Around three-thirty, a student or a co-worker will come to draw with him, or he drives out to a construction site.

His method of working would definitely not be taken seriously by many architects, and yet it is more productive than an office with a large staff.

One of my girlfriends, who had been working until recently in an architect's office in Munich and who is now working for Loos says: "Loos easily designs in half an hour what we often needed to spend weeks and months on in the office."

A young student of Loos, who had come right out of technical school, said after two months: "I have now learned more with Loos than I did during four years at technical school!"

The final drawings for the interior remodelling are made right at the carpenter's, in the room next to the workshop, and oftentimes the advice of the carpenter himself will be sought.

The best building designs by Loos, however, originate on the marble tops of coffee house tables.

MENUS...

The menus at Loos' are as international as the man himself. As part of the daily fare one finds:

"Pot-au-feu." Meat is cooked over a flame with lots of vegetables and spices. For example, mutton with cabbage or a stewing hen with a lot of vegetables, mushrooms and spices. If there are any leftovers, then a new vegetable is added to the pot, if there are still leftovers from the vegetable, then new meat is added and cooked.

Loos says: "'Pot-au-feu' is better on the second day than on the first, on the third better than on the second." A French tale claims that Henry IV supposedly kept this dish going for more than 120 years!

This dish is a real lifesaver for dear Mitzi. Loos often brings many unexpected guests at the last minute, so the "pot-au-feu" is usually all gone by the third day.

*

Another item of daily fare is porridge, prepared the English way:

Two coffee cups of oatmeal are sprinkled into three coffee cups of boiling water, cooked a few minutes, but not too long. "The flakes should indeed be soft, yet still lie individually on top of each other," says Loos. Cream and sugar are served separately with this dish.

Loos takes only a small portion on his plate, pours lots of cream over it and sprinkles sugar on top. "One has to be able to crunch on the sugar," he says.

Loos has long discussions with General K. in Prague who is of the same opinion as Loos that this healthy dish should be introduced into the Army; of course, milk would have to be used instead of cream.

The attempt fails; the soldiers do not like porridge.

*

Spinach or Savoy cabbage is washed well, cooked in water, put without any lard into a open saucepan for a minute to let the water evaporate, only then a bit of butter or lard is added.

Loos says: "Creamed spinach is only made so that one won't notice that it wasn't washed well!"

*

Before the soup, raw carrots that have been washed, cut lengthwise and placed in a water-glass on the table, are often eaten.

*

Schnitzel should never be pounded. Loos says: "The juice, the best part, gets beaten out!"

GROUNDS FOR DIVORCE

Loos enters the bathroom. His face grows red with anger. "You want to be my wife?" he shouts, "you, who have no respect for material? Who senselessly wastes it, lets it melt into nothing? You squanderer, you! Don't you know that I have spent my entire life fighting against the senseless, against ornamentation, against the waste of energy, against the waste of material? And you, my wife, dare to let this wonderful soap senselessly dissolve in the water?"

ONE SHOULD NOT PUT
ONE'S MONEY IN THE BANK

I had never spoken to Loos about money matters. Still, I did dare once to timidly ask: "Dolfi, where do you have an account?" Loos looked at me in amazement. "Account? In a bank, so that I have to pay taxes? No, I prefer to spend my money myself... Whenever I get some, I put it in my coat pocket and spend it. That is what it's for!"

"But Dolf," I say cautiously, "there isn't any more money in your coat pocket."

"Well, well," Loos says and takes out his wallet. "Yes, yes, you are right... I did not even notice. Then write immediately to our housekeeper, Mitzi, she should go and get some money. And my student, Kulka... Lerle," he cried out beaming. "I still have one hundred crowns there, and you tell me we have no money! We will go out for a nice lunch today!"

I do not find this at all reassuring. "But if Mitzi does not send us any money and Kulka doesn't either, what will we do then?"

Dolf shrugs his shoulders, irritated. "Just as God will not let the sparrows on the roof starve to death, he will not let me starve to death either... My student Zladko Neumann, with whom I lived in Paris, asked me the same question once. All of our resources were used up, we each had only three francs... Zladko was desperate, but I told him the same I told you. Then we each bought a bottle of wine for two francs fifty and lay down in bed. That way we saved on heating, since it was winter. The next day a letter came from Kuhner, my client, with the following content:

'Dear Loos! All of my friends who had their homes remodelled at the same time that I did have since had them remodelled three or four times while I am so satisfied with my apartment, which you did 25 years ago, that I hope to spend another fifty in it. Not only have you saved me a great deal of money but my apartment is more beautiful and more modern than those of my friends. I therefore beg you to accept the amount of 25,000 crowns, which I honestly feel I owe you. Yours thankfully...'

"You can imagine how we felt when that letter arrived. Zladko was quite beside himself... We immediately arranged for big party of course... The entire Montparnasse was invited – all the poor artists who had been starving just as we had. Also the young girls who were freezing on the street corners, a few countesses and counts and very rich people who were quite shocked at the company, but stayed anyway. In reality they were just happy to have a good time. Yes, and the 25,000 crowns? Yes, Lerle, quite a large part of it had of course disappeared by that time...

But I got more work soon after that. I just want to prove to you that my dear God does not abandon me. I am not afraid...

"And you, because you are my wife, do not need to be afraid either!"

Two days later, Kulka sent the amount of two thousand crowns.

The thought of having a divinely-favored husband, who would never be forsaken by his Savior, was certainly uplifting, but it still did not satisfy my innate sense of practicality. What if this God ever did fail...! I decided to open an account at the next opportunity.

The next time we were in the city, we visited a client who, like all his clients, received Loos as his dear friend. Loos took him into the next room and whispered to him a while. He then came back in a good mood. I found in the afternoon his wallet again full.

"Just think," said Loos, "the good man immediately gave me some money when I asked for it."

"And you took it?"

"Of course!"

So it had come to the point that Loos would simply go and ask his clients for money – charity!

Loos, who noticed I was upset, looked at me in amazement: "You think this is charity? No! All... All my clients owe me money! ... Think of the story I told you recently, the story that took place in Paris... But not just my clients, the whole world owes me money, because I have freed it from ornamentation, from unnecessary work! What the city of Vienna alone has saved by no longer having to nail ornaments onto the local council buildings, cannot even be expressed in money... They all owe me money," he continued murmuring before he lapsed into his midday nap...

*

I, however, was not satisfied with this answer. I tried to gain a better understanding of his business practices. Loos adapted his work according to the means of his clients. He was capable too, of creating something absolutely beautiful for little money. Loos was not only a great interior designer, he had an exceptional knowledge of materials as well. For example, he would not hesitate to go out himself to select wood paneling for his clients instead of leaving it to his carpenters. He carefully chose pieces with the most beautiful wood grain. That way, even less expensive kinds of wood would not look lesser. (As a rule, however, he disliked Caucasian nut and rosewood and never used them.)

Loos also preferred to work with ordinary craftsmen, who were inexpensive and with whom he could get along better than with cabinet-makers or engineers. Loos felt a strong human bond with these simple, good people, and they in turn considered Loos, despite their admiration for his great art, as one of them.

Loos knew of many small shops where one could buy valuable carpets, beautiful vases, lamps and other items for little money. It was always a great pleasure for him to take a client there and explain the value or worthlessness of individual items with everything right there.

Finally, Loos always thanked his client over and over for having given him the opportunity to realize one of his artistic ideas. He received as honorarium the usual 10 percent. But Loos usually went to his client whenever he needed money and so when work on a project was completed, he was not owed any more.

I succeeded in putting money into a bank instead of into his coat pocket. I just wanted to have a little security. I started to carry money over to the bank. Loos did not object. Money in a bank – that was something new! Sometimes, early in the morning, he would dress quickly and leave, whistling.

"Where are you going, Dolf?"

Loos, beaming: "To the bank, to get some money!"

Things continued like that for a while, the money in the bank started to dwindle, and one day there was nothing left.

"Why isn't there any more money in the bank?" Loos said, quite surprised, "you did put it in there!"

He thought one could now go and get money for an unlimited time.

"Or did the tax authorities confiscate the money?" he asked suspiciously. "See, I told you right off. One should not put one's money in the bank..."

MARBLE

Every marble that Loos uses has a story. This one I experienced first-hand:

Loos visits a marble quarry in Switzerland. Here he finds, carelessly rolled aside, blocks of Cipolino marble. It is brittle stone because streaks of foreign metal ores run through it. Loos, however, knows that this diseased marble in particular is incredibly beautiful. He wants to buy it; it costs almost nothing. Since Loos has no money at all, he convinces a client to buy it. The buyer is quite astonished when four blocks instead of three arrive from Switzerland. The following note is enclosed: "Dear Herr B.! We took the liberty of sending a fourth block along for free since it was just lying in our way..." There is so much marble that Loos, who had planned on paneling his client's dining room with it, changes his mind. "It would be a shame," he says, "only to use part of it."

A year passes. Loos builds the Müller house in Prague. Dr. Müller buys the marble for the large hall. Tumultuous days follow – the marble specialists in Prague refuse to cut the stone. They are afraid it will break – Loos will not give up. Finally, an Italian says he is willing to take over the job, although without a guarantee. Loos says the stone will have to be put onto concrete slabs and pieced together if it breaks.

Despite his optimism Loos is very nervous. One day passes, a second – will it work, will it not work? It works! The Italian informs us. The slabs have been cut, only a few show cracks, splits. Most of them are whole. Loos rejoices. We immediately take the car to the workshop. The slabs are lying there on long tables, but they are gray and colourless! I am disappointed. Loos, however, laughs. They have not been polished yet. Look! He takes some water and pours it over the gray stone. A miracle occurs! The wet marble gleams a deep green; blue, violet and reddish-yellow veins of colour run through it in soft waves. It looks like the sea.

A VISIT TO FRAU X.

Shortly after we are married we visit Frau X. She is a good friend of Loos and one of his benefactors. I have read and heard a lot about her and have always wanted very much to meet her. I make myself look particularly nice. A black velvet dress... and I finish by donning a little hat with a veil.

A number of prominent people are here as guests. Frau X. is like a queen at her court, she leads the discussion, bringing individuals into the conversation as she sees fit. Is it just an accident or is it on purpose? She ignores me, as if I were not there. The conversation is light and witty, it jumps from person to person. I try to join in... I fail, Frau X. immediately cuts me off... So I sit, lonely and abandoned, fighting back my tears...

My husband is deeply involved in a discussion with an artist. Since he is hard of hearing, any conversation is difficult, I do not want to disturb him. Time passes... Finally we leave. At home I throw myself on the bed crying my heart out.

"Oh Lerle, oh Lerle," he says, "what happened?"

"You know," I sob, "I realize that next to you I am nothing, but at Frau X.'s I was less than nothing!"

My husband sits beside me and gently strokes my hair.

"Don't let it bother you, Lerle! When I was there with Elsie, when I was there with Bessie, when I was there with Lina, my wives always came back home crying... Don't let it get to you, Lerle, she is only jealous I didn't also marry her!"

NEWSPAPERS

Loos sits for hours on end buried in his newspapers and is not available to talk to anyone. He reads English, French and German newspapers, although he does not understand much French. He reads the newspaper with the same attention from beginning to end, only leaving out the novel section. He says: "Studying the classified ads is just as important as reading the political news. From them you learn the needs and the surpluses of a country."

WHY DO YOU ONLY WANT A BED?

"Dolfi, why don't you want a couch in the bedroom, why only a bed?"

"The bed, Lerle, the bedroom is the most sacred, most private matter, no stranger should be allowed to profane this sanctuary... The bedroom should not have a door opening onto a living room!"

"But Dolfi, if there is very little room in an apartment?"

"Then the bedroom should be very small... Just enough room for a double bed... The closets are built in or placed in the hallway."

"But if there isn't any room for them either?"

Dolf looks up annoyed from his newspaper. His glasses have slid down his nose. "Let me read, Lerle, take the dog for a walk!"

THE DIFFERENCE

I have a terrible mess in my room. When I return from a walk, I find Loos standing in the middle of the still un-tidied room. He looks at me and asks:

"Do you know the essential difference between a proletarian and an aristocrat?

I silently shake my head.

"A proletarian leaves everything lying around. He says: the personnel is there to tidy up. An aristocrat puts everything away himself, it is embarrassing for him to have a stranger, an employee, handle his private things..."

THE MÜLLER HOUSE

The Müller house is growing. Loos orders an overhang of a half a centimeter on the house. He drives away. When he returns, the overhang measures an entire centimeter instead of only a half. Loos is beside himself and has the extra half a centimeter taken off all the way around the house. To the left of the main entrance is a door. In this room, the master of the house can receive visitors whom he does not wish to take into the house. Here there is a desk, a bench, the room is covered in dark lilac wallpaper; a large space is left un-papered, and this is where Loos had a gigantic map put up. A lovely, colourful interruption – and at the same time a guest who is waiting can pass the time pleasantly.

A double glass door leads into the front hall, which is panelled in white wood. The ceiling is low; Loos, however, still finds it too high and so has it painted dark blue at the last minute. A nice contrast to the white wood. Now come three, four steps. Then, an overwhelming sight – the large main room. Loos has intentionally made the entrance intimate and low so that the impact of the main room is intensified. He says it is wrong, when one opens the door, to immediately, without a transition, be standing in the largest room of the house. To the left, situated between two blocks of green marble, is a sofa covered in lilac upholstery. On top of each of the marble blocks, which house the heating, Loos had wanted to put an old Japanese wooden figurine, but he found none that he would have liked. The client has a whole life ahead of him, he has time "to grow into" the house and has room to acquire many beautiful objects that will fit into the house. That is what Loos thinks, and so he gives up the search for the wooden figurines.

A narrow staircase in the main room leads up to the boudoir. A window looks down from this room into the main room so that the lady of the house can observe those arriving without herself being noticed. A small, delicate woman, she will make a grand and imposing impression as she walks down the stairs toward her guests.

On the right side of the main room, a couple of steps lead up to a dining room. The extra space that this has created under the dining room allows for light from the street to reach the utility rooms in the cellar. The ceiling of the dining room is made of dark mahogany. A subsequent client also wanted to have such a ceiling in his dining room. Loos said: "I was able to put a wood ceiling in this small room because it opens out onto the main room. In a small, enclosed room, this ceiling would look like the lid of a coffin. I'll make your ceiling run through the dining room and the men's sitting room, then it is possible." (Loos did, as a matter of fact, connect the men's sitting room and the dining room in this new apartment and put up a continuous mahogany ceiling, which looked wonderful.)

Dr. Müller's dining room is, like all Loos' dining rooms, not very large. Loos says: "It is large enough as long as the maid can comfortably serve a meal. There is no need for more room than that." The round granite table required a lot of planning. It was constructed in such a way that with a few guests one round mahogany tabletop could be put out, and two tabletops when there were more guests. The chairs are copies of Chippendale chairs.

Next to the dining room is a small room, the pantry, and then comes the kitchen; it is surprisingly small. Cooking is done here following the American system. Everything is within easy reach and has its own designated place. Loos uses the kitchen of a dining car as a model. A light is installed above the stove. The window is high. Loos explains, smiling: "It is unnecessary for the cook to be able to look out of the window while cooking."

When the house was completed, the following article appeared in the *Prager Tagblatt* on February 15, 1931:

"During the past three months, the Müller house, located across from the Norbert Church in Štřeschowitz, has become a popular place to visit. It was built by Adolf Loos. The guest book boasts such names as Marcel Ray, Karl

Kraus, Emil Ludwig, Machar, Filene, Ilja Ehrenburg, and Arnold Schönberg. Karin Michaelis wrote the following to Loos after having toured the house: "Dear friend, the house in Prague is by far, far, far the most beautiful one that you have built. If there were such a thing as a precious stone that was more elegant and more valuable than diamonds, emeralds or sapphires, I would compare this house with it. If I were Kokoschka, I would want to paint twelve pictures in it, if I were Pavlova, I would only want to dance there."

AT THE NUDIST BATHHOUSE

Frau Erna calls me on the telephone and asks: "Wouldn't you like to go bathing with us today? We are going to the Strohgasse... Do bring your husband along too!"

"Strohgasse?" says Loos, immediately knitting his brows. "You want to go bathing with a bunch of lunatics? That's that nudist club bathhouse..."

"If Erna is going," I reply, my curiosity peaking, " it is definitely healthy, moral and nice."

"Healthy, moral perhaps... but nice?! Brrr..." Loos shudders with disgust. "I have never seen such a group of tense, unnatural people as I have there... And yet they only carry on extremely moral conversations. The slightest flirting is forbidden... The whole thing is hypocritical and unnatural, nowhere have I ever found such a strained conversational tone. The people there all think they are so superior because they talk about art, literature and the theater while in the nude. Those are not natural, free human beings at all, just undressed Philistines!"

"Just don't talk to them then," I plead, "I would like so much to see these strange people."

"Alright," says Loos, suddenly staring at me with a serious, wide-eyed look, "we will go. But I am warning you: there will be no backing out, that will be your punishment!"

We go. I am already feeling a tremendous urge to run when a red-haired, skinny, hunchbacked man, who is wearing less than nothing, hospitably shows us to the changing rooms.

"You will hardly find any beauties here," Loos whispers to me, "ugly people have the peculiar trait of wanting to be seen in the nude."

I am searching desperately for an excuse to leave. Loos, who has suspected this, forces me to stay by giving me a stern look.

Thank God, there is something resembling a towel in the dressing room. I wrap myself up tightly in it, determined not to give up this utensil without a fight. I leave the room feeling a little more self-confident.

Loos walks towards me dressed in paradisiacal garb so totally at ease and comfortable as if he were wearing a fine well-tailored suit. He casts me a scathing, disparaging look but does not say anything.

We enter the bathing hall. Groups of nothing less than beautiful people, some sitting on benches, some standing, women and men, seem to be carrying on profound conversations. Their facial expressions are serious and dignified but their poses seem curiously chosen and their voices agitated. They look like bad extras to me. Noticing us come in, their eyes fall on us, and reluctantly settle on me. I am dying of embarrassment and wrap myself up even tighter in my towel.

"You are causing an unpleasant scene with your towel," Loos says scornfully, "just drop it and no one will stare at you anymore. Here among the nudists you have the same effect as a naked person among the clothed!"

Sure enough, as soon as I drop my towel all eyes turn away indifferently and pay me no more attention. Loos pulls me into the water. His face brightens when he sees a young blond man. It is our journeyman carpenter Josef.

"How lucky to meet you here," exclaims Loos; not in the least embarrassed, he genially extends his hand. "I had wanted to go the workshop today anyway. Are the veneers finished yet?"

The carpenter nods. "May I introduce you? Josef – my wife!"

Since I am not particularly thrilled by this introduction, I head back to dry land while Loos continues his discussion of the veneers. Distraught, I pace back and forth. Thank God, Erna comes towards me. She ceremoniously introduces me to a few people and offers me a cigarette. The red-headed hunchbacked man shows up again. He looks at me with a scathing gaze.

"You really ought to enroll in one of our exercise classes," he says in a high falsetto voice, "I can see several fat deposits on you."

I force myself to a polite smile even though I feel rather like crying. Luckily, Erna has initiated a conversation about art and literature. I try to also express my opinion, everyone listens politely, yet I have the feeling that no one really cares at all about me.

Loos climbs out of the water. He remains standing a long while on the top step, slowly and carefully removing the water off his body so as not to carry any more water into the dressing room than is absolutely necessary. He then motions to me to do the same.

"I am really very glad," he says cheerily, "we came here, otherwise I would not have gotten to meet the carpenter. And you," he continues, "did you have a good time?"

I remain silent. Loos makes an innocent face and whistles to himself.

THE COMPANIONWAY

Loos meets client X. on the street. "Just imagine," he exclaims, "a visitor to my villa yesterday complained about the narrow staircase, and do you know what he compared it with? A ship's companionway!"

"With a companionway?" Loos cries out excitedly. "Did he really say that? When you see that man again, shake his hand for me and tell him someone has finally really understood my architecture. The ship is the model for a modern house. There, space is totally utilized, no unnecessary waste of space! Nowadays, with building sites being so expensive, every inch of space must be used... I have not only got rid of ornamentation, I have discovered a new way of building. Building into space, the Raumplan, spatial design. I do not build in flat planes, I build in space, in three-dimensions. This is the way I manage to accommodate more rooms into a house. The bathroom does not need to have a ceiling as high as the living room... The rooms are nested into each other, each has a height and size corresponding to its purpose. The staircase, however, connects the separate, different levels... A person has to be able to walk comfortably... a staircase is not made so that couples go rushing past each other. It does not need to be any wider than a ship's companionway...

"Unfortunately the architects of today don't know yet how to think in terms of space. In a hundred years it will be different! Seven hundred years ago there was a man who could think in terms of space – it was Dante in his 'Divine Comedy'..."

LOOS IS ILL

Loos is ill. We have not heard anything from Karl Kraus for weeks. Suddenly he calls from Berlin. He asks how Loos is feeling. He does not call just once, he calls daily.

A few weeks later, Kraus is in Vienna. He drops by daily at seven in the evening to see Loos. "At breakfast time," jokes Loos, since Kraus sleeps during the day and works at night.

During this period all other visitors must be kept away. Loos is happy to see Kraus so often. He says: "I did not know at all that Kraus has such a Jewish sense of family."

"But Dolf, you are not even at all related to him." *

Loos nods, annoyed: "Oh, but I am, I am... a relative by choice..."

---

* In fact, through his marriage to Claire, Loos did become related to Kraus, whose youngest brother Alfred was married to Otto Beck's cousin, Rosa Hirsch. The Hirsches were also Pilsen clients of Loos and became the subjects of several well-known Kokoschka paintings.

IT IS NOT THAT EASY

We are walking down the Kärntnerstrasse. I contemplatively watch the girls strolling by. This irritates Loos.

"Yes, yes, you middleclass women think the life these girls lead is so easy! One of you should try standing out here and asking for 100 schillings... you would soon find out something... You can always find someone to go with you for free... but for money – – –?!"

A TOTAL MESS AND AN HONORARY GRAVE

Loos is still sick. The doctors find his condition very serious. We take him to a well-known Viennese sanatorium. The ward rounds are at 5 o'clock.

"How are you feeling here with us?" asks the head physician.

"A total mess," says Loos, his voice dying away.

The head physician looks at the junior physician, the junior physician at the assistant and the assistant at the nurse. She helplessly shrugs her shoulders.

"Yes, yes, a total mess – this place is like the Balkans!" exclaims Loos loudly. "I'm just surprised they don't put roux in the compote."

"What on earth has happened?" asks the astounded head physician.

Loos replies, "They serve hot milk with your tea here!"

The doctor orders Loos a sedative.

From now on, however, cold milk is served with tea throughout the entire sanatorium...

Loos' condition worsens. One day he asks me to give him a sheet of paper and a pencil. With a great deal of effort and a trembling hand he draws a block on it and writes beneath it: 'Born Brünn, died Vienna.' Look, Lerle, this is my tombstone!"

"How can one be having such depressing thoughts?!" To cheer him up, I draw four little blocks around the first and write the names of his wives on them.

Loos looks at the drawing and says with a fading voice, "Not even when I am dead can I expect to be left in peace?!"

He takes a fresh sheet of paper and sketches a new block on it. Then he presses the drawing into my hand and dictates to me short and to the point: "Tombstone of gray granite; size,..." – Loos thinks for a moment –, "size not specified, it depends on how much money is available... It should not be too small though or it will look like an over-sized inkwell, and," he adds in conclusion, "write *Ehrengrab* [honorary grave] on it!"

I look at Loos for a moment, astonished. Loos, who has guessed my thoughts, smiles. I can see in his eyes that the old rogue is being sarcastic and cynical. "Just write down honorary grave. The Viennese are going to have such a bad conscience when it comes to me that I am sure I will get an honorary grave!"

With that he turns himself over towards the wall, five minutes later he has fallen asleep. The very next day he regains his health.

THE ENCYCLOPEDIA

"What are you looking up in the encyclopedia, Dolfi?"

"I'm not looking up anything."

"What are you doing then?"

"I'm reading."

"In the encyclopedia?"

"Yes, it's the most interesting reading material I know of. Far more interesting than any old novel!"

LOOS SAYS...

"Little has changed in my architecture over 30 years. But I am a lot shorter, just as the earlier car differentiates itself from that of today mainly in that it is a lot lower."

"I am a Communist. The difference between me and a Bolshevik is only that I want to turn all the people into aristocrats, whereas he wants to turn them all into proletarians..."

When one of his female clients asks during a discussion about her dining room decor if Loos wouldn't consider making the buffet a little larger, Loos answers: "That is what you want? I find that the larger the buffet, the more stupid is the woman!"

Loos is sitting having dinner with one of his female admirers. Suddenly she says: "Oh, forgive me, Herr Loos, I drank out of your glass by mistake."

Loos replies perfectly straight-faced: "That is quite alright, dear Frau X., I am not terrified of anything!"

AT PENSION Z. IN VIENNA...

We are sitting at the big communal table of the hotel. And facing us is a lady with her grown-up daughter. They bow their heads way down over their plates. They slurp their soup. I can tell that Loos finds this visibly disturbing. The meat is served... The two ladies hold their knife close to the blade. They spread out their elbows.

Loos mumbles: "So that they won't cut their fingers."

The meat has been eaten, but some gravy remains. Then something terrible happens: Using their knives, the ladies slurp up the gravy.

Loos cannot contain himself any longer. "I fear, dear madam, that you are going to cut your mouth," and with a face permeated with the seriousness of a holy mission, he begins: "Years ago I published an article called 'The Introduction of Occidental Culture into Austria,' you should read it... By the way, where do you come from anyway?"

"I'm Turkish."

Loos breathes a sigh of relief: "Lucky for you!"

THE MANDL HOUSE

Herr Mandl tells me how his house came to be. "I was thinking," says Herr Mandl, "about buying some real estate in the Blaasgasse but I couldn't make up my mind. An acquaintance gave me the advice I should look up Adolf Loos. Loos drove out to Döbling with me, looked at the house and simply said: 'Buy it, by all means, buy it.' I still could not decide, however, as the house was old, a real shambles. I visited Loos again. I asked: 'Just why should I buy this house?' Loos replied: 'The location is good, I have some new ideas precisely for this project.' Loos takes a paper napkin and sketches on it. 'First of all, the guts of the house have to be removed. Everything inside will have to go. The right exterior wall of the house will have to be removed.' We immediately started work on the house. It's standing there, with only three walls. It was late in the fall, construction was halted. Loos left for Nice. It rained, it snowed, it stormed. In the spring, Loos returns, construction is resumed. 'I get my best ideas when I'm building – I never make plans.' He creates a palatial hall that rises up two stories high –, the house is unrecognizable.

"One day Loos is sitting across from me at the desk and stares at me for a long while. Finally, he says: 'I know now how the interior will have to look. For you there is only one material: oak.' I jump up, saying: 'Herr Architect, may I say *du* to you? Do you know I have always loved oak?' Loos hugs me and says: 'I have known that already for the longest time; you do not need to tell me.' But then I became again a little anxious. Won't it cost a fortune? Loos: 'You will get that amount back many times over if you ever sell the house, and then I will build you a new, even far more beautiful one.' Loos would be proven right. I sold the house for many times over what I paid for it.

"But there were a few differences between us. I had some antique furniture and a few works by Kolo Moser. I furnished the upstairs rooms with them. Loos did not like these pieces at all. If visitors were at the house, and Loos were present, he would never fail to mention in a most disapproving tone: 'These people already had this furniture.' Originally, he wanted to have the columns in the dining room constructed out of rough brick. I would not agree to it and so marble columns were put in. Loos sighed when he saw them and said: 'I never should have given in; rough brick would have created an entirely different effect.' But the hall made of polished light oak looked stunning. I am convinced that my house is the most beautiful of all, in the end it had become what both of us had imagined. Loos was not my architect, I was not his client – we built it together."

THE CARINTHIAN BALL IN VIENNA

"Lerle, let's go; Mitzi, our housekeeper Mitzi, is on the organizing committee and is getting us a large private box. You know, Lerle, that Mitzi would be very offended if we didn't go; we only need to stay half an hour, we owe that much to our Mitzi."

I am wearing a red and white checked Dirndl, Dolfi a brown leather jacket. Mitzi greets us in a Carinthian folk costume, it looks wonderful on her.

"I never realized that she is so beautiful," Dolf whispers to me.

The folk costume procession is colourful and lively. We are sitting in the private box with Mitzi's husband, who is a specialist in refrigerators, his nephew, an apprentice carpenter, a retailer of fancy foods, a charming young girl and a waitress. Dolfi is in the best of moods.

The folk costume procession breaks up into dance couples. I start to get up and want to leave, as agreed. Dolfi's eyes are still enthusiastically fixed on individual country beauties.

"I have been to a lot of balls, but I have never seen so much natural beauty anywhere!" he exclaims. "None of them are wearing any make-up, many of them look so elegant that the city girls can just run and hide." He would not dream of leaving now. A good-looking tall country lad asks me for a dance. I glance over to my husband, he nods. "Go ahead and dance, Lerle, have a good time!"

The young man is a shoemaker and asks me where I am working. I say that I am a waitress here in Vienna. The young man asks me for a second dance. I quickly glance over at our table, Loos has disappeared. I am not worried and continue dancing. The shoemaker comes over again and again, asking me to dance, my face is getting red from lying. Then Mitzi approaches.

"Madame," she calls out from a distance, "and oh God, Franzl!", before I can say anything, Franzl now realizes who I am and, upset, quickly disappears.

"Where is my husband?" I ask. Mitzi does not know. We go through the ballrooms searching for him. Finally, in the last one, we find him sitting, a pretty girl from Mondsee on each side. Sitting in the corner are two lads glaring in anger at Loos. He sees us and waves.

"You know, Lerle, we absolutely have to go to Mondsee sometime soon," he says beaming. "In the spring they have a big festival, a real Walpurgisnacht. People jump through the bonfires, they bake a special kind of cake... Lerle, we really have to go there!" Then to the two girls: "Tomorrow, ladies, you must both come over to my house for lunch, you don't mind, do you, Lerle?" I indicate I do not.

At this point, one of the country lads jumps up, furiously pounding his fist on the table. "But we mind, that girl you're flirting with is my fiancée, sir!"

Indignant, the girl jumps up. "This man was behaving very properly!"

"Sure, but he was talkin' to you the whole time!"

"That's because he's smarter than you are, you stupid lout!"

And then all hell breaks loose! Mitzi and I grab Dolf under each arm and quickly usher him outside.

"What happened, Lerle?" he asks, because he did not hear. "Why doesn't she want to come for lunch?... Why?"

CHAIRS

"We do not have any good chairs," Loos often says. He tries once himself to design a chair – it fails. He suggests that Thonet sponsor a chair-designing contest. Thonet follows his advice, but does not choose Loos to be a juror. This upsets Loos.

Loos does not like furniture made of steel. He tolerates it for the waiting room of a doctor's office or in a shoe store but never uses it himself. It is too mechanical for his taste. Loos remarks sarcastically: "A new discovery has been made in Central Europe. Metal chairs! How ridiculous! Even the good old French king Dagobert had a throne constructed according to the same principles of this 'new invention'. But the era of monarchs is long since gone. One can see that even in art by the fact that a Ludwig II of Bavaria was no longer capable of forcing someone like Richard Wagner onto the stupid masses, whereas in the old days, the sovereign imposed on the population the artists of his liking."

Loos took me once to an old church in Nancy. He showed me the chair of an ecclesiastical prince – it was made out of metal! He is constantly occupied with the chair problem. What he would really like is to have Japanese basket weavers come to Europe and have them weave him some chairs. But it would cost too much. Loos uses English chairs in his dining rooms, Chippendales. Since his chair-maker died though, he cannot find anyone who can really copy Chippendales well.

We are in Hall. Loos is sitting in front of the hotel. Suddenly he becomes excited – jumps up –, closely examines the wicker chair, sits down again testing it – gets up again! An inscription on the back of the chair reads: Herlitz, Scharnstein. Loos waves down a cab. "Lerle, get in." We drive to Scharnstein. Herr Herlitz is a simple man. Loos looks over all of his furniture. "Good, good," he says. On a tabletop, he draws the new chair – without any arms. A model is made. Loos is not satisfied. It takes three or four additional models before he is finally pleased. He has the seat and back of the chair covered in coloured oilcloth upholstery. The edge of the upholstery is finished off with a row of round-headed tacks, making it look like a fine gold chain. Loos places these wicker chairs, each upholstered in a different colour, in a dining room with yellow travertine marble.

EVERYONE SHOULD BE HIS OWN BOSS

Loos says: "I'm against any kind of political party; against partisanship. The city housing projects are only built in order to promote party support. The people get herded together so they will vote for the party.

"Everyone should have his own little house and his own garden. Rental property should be reserved solely for businesses. In England, they have already created business districts in the cities; the people live in cottages in the suburbs. Business hours are from 9 to 4 and after that everyone is his own boss. Humankind will not be truly happy until it can live like that. Rich and poor; the lower middle-class worker has his own little house just like the rich businessman... and everyone is his own boss. That is how things should be!"

EMIL LUDWIG IN PRAGUE

"Lerle, Emil Ludwig is in Prague, go see him, send him my best regards and ask him if he would like to take a tour of my house here in Prague."

"Dolfi, I can't do that; I don't even know Emil Ludwig!"

Loos is not feeling very well. He sits up in bed, his eyes are fixed on me.

"What can't you do, Lerle?"

I stutter: "Simply go visit the famous Emil Ludwig..."

"Lerle, shame on you, you never want to do anything for me anymore. You're lazy, so lazy!" He sighs.

"Well, I will gladly go, but will he even agree to see me?"

Loos is truly angry. "If you tell him you are my wife, definitely! – By the way, he's an old friend of mine. Dolfi chuckles softly to himself. "I remember, it's been several years now, he turned up once in our circle. Emil Ludwig! Karl Kraus said about him: 'He's dark and soft like a Blüthner grand piano.' We did not take him very seriously. Yes, Lerle, back then he wasn't any older than you... He later visited me one more time with his wife. Rumor had it in Vienna that she was an English aristocrat. Do you remember that little book with the Scottish tartan plaids in it? Every aristocrat has one of those patterns in his family crest. I wanted to really please her so I handed her the book and said, 'Surely your crest is in there too.' She looked at it astonished because she was no aristocrat! The Viennese had been grossly exaggerating as usual. But do go now, Lerle. I'm tired and want to sleep."

My nervousness has strangely disappeared. "Just tell me, please, why I should actually show Emil Ludwig the house?"

Loos is very surprised by my question. "But Lerle, didn't you say yourself that Emil Ludwig is a famous man? All prominent people of our time should see my house."

I go to the Hotel Steiner and leave my calling card. A short while later, a tall, black-haired man with a very pleasant, soft voice does indeed appear.

"Madame, how very nice to see you again. Excuse me," he says, as I come closer, "You're not at all the Frau Loos I know." It turned out he had thought I was Lina, Loos' first wife. "And how is Loos doing?" he asks cordially, after the mistake has been cleared up, "I have not seen him in twenty-five years."

A little embarrassed, I excuse his absence with his illness. We take a cab and drive to the Müller villa that Loos built in Prague. On the way, I have a wonderful idea: Emil Ludwig writes the memoirs of famous men, so couldn't he write a Loos biography?... Stuttering and clumsy, I make my proposal. Emil Ludwig knits his brow, then gently shakes his head, and replies in his soft voice:

"Loos... Loos is not famous enough... he's no Napoleon."

"No, that he is not," I think bitterly to myself, "he has not killed anyone, all he has ever wanted is to free people from the burden of unnecessary labor..." The rest of the drive to the villa is marked by an uncomfortable atmosphere. Luckily we arrive at the house before too long. In silence, we tour the rooms. Out on the terrace, from which one can see all of Prague, we remain standing for a long, long time.

Then Emil Ludwig says slowly, "It is too bad they just finished my house in Switzerland.... Really too bad! I should have had Loos build it..."

"Well, Lerle, how was it, how did Emil Ludwig like my house?"

I tell him all about the visit.

"Yes, Lerle, " says Loos, as I have finished telling him, "someday a lot of people will regret that they did not have me build them a house, but by that time it will definitely be too late!" He sighs... Suddenly he turns to me, "I hope that in your enthusiasm you did not talk him into writing a biography about me! I would gladly build him a house, but if he ever wrote a biography about me, I could never forgive him!"

LOOS AND THOMAS BAŤA

Loos wants to found a school for architecture. Five prominent men are to sign a petition: Heinrich Mann, Valéry Larbaud, Arnold Schönberg, Karl Kraus and, as the fifth, Loos would like to have Baťa. Loos considers him one of the most influential men of our time... But Baťa refuses. Loos wires him, calls him on the telephone, to no avail... Baťa refuses. Loos feels very insulted. He says: "I'll never forgive him for this!"

We are sitting in the Mánes Restaurant in Prague. Baťa is at the next table. Loos jumps up. Even though he does not know him personally, nevertheless he rushes right over to him. "Why didn't you sign the petition for the school?"

Baťa makes an unassuming gesture as if to say, it would be a great honor for me, but I am, after all, just a simple man! Loos: "I've seen your factory – one of the greatest plants there is anywhere! You are a real philanthropist! Everyone should take a trip to Zlín and see your factory. You are a master of organization... You could be a government leader!" He shakes Baťa's hand in recognition. But Baťa remains unmoved. He doesn't sign.

When we are alone again, I ask Loos: "Why don't you actually wear any shoes from Baťa?" Loos makes a guilty face. "You know I never wear ready-made clothes!"

COLOURS

Loos says: "I do not understand architects! They are always afraid of using strong colours beside each other.

"I find that a meadow full of flowers is very beautiful, and yet every flower is a different colour.

"Colours can be used together in a room in exactly the same way as long as they are as pure as the colours of a meadow of flowers. It is only the blended colours, the dirtied colours, that are not pretty..."

I AM A COSMOPOLITAN

A big exhibition is being held abroad. Loos is also represented. His plans are exhibited alongside the work of the Austrian artists. Loos does not know anything about the whole affair. His student, Kulka, in Vienna, had sent in the plans. We happen to be in Prague and Loos is attacked by the Czechoslovak artists.

"You are a Czechoslovak, Loos, how is it that are you are exhibiting with the Austrians, it has caused a lot of ill will here. You are losing your popularity with the people here by doing this!"

Loos, who has no idea of what they are talking about, has the situation explained to him first, then he replies, shaking his head: "The Czechoslovaks think I am a Czechoslovak because I was born in Brno and came from there. The Austrians say I've lived in Vienna for so many years, the Germans say I am German because I speak their language, in France, they suggested that I become a naturalized citizen because I love their country so much, my English wife always said I dressed better than an Englishman...," and smiling: "I am neither one nor the other. I am a cosmopolitan, as is every true European..."

THE SIXTIETH BIRTHDAY
(December 10, 1930)

Loos' sixtieth birthday is celebrated in Prague. The citizens of Prague are particularly proud of the fact that Loos, the great Loos, is a Czechoslovak citizen and will not be denied the opportunity to honor him in a grand manner.

Dr. Markalous, the Czechoslovak journalist and writer, has made arrangements for a celebration in the Společenský club. A large tea party takes place.

Loos is ceremoniously welcomed and handed a bouquet of red roses. Suddenly, on the threshold to the banquet hall, Loos stops.

"Quick, Lerle, go back to the Hotel Steiner and get Karl Kraus. He will not come on his own, he hates public celebrations... I would really like for him to be here."

Just at that moment a fanfare sounds and the doors open, it is out of the question now for me to leave. We walk in. But right beside the door, amid the other guests, stands Karl Kraus.

We are led to two chairs, thrones of a sort.

One architect gives a speech and is followed by a second. Loos can tell by the way they move their mouths that the one is speaking German and the other Czech. He interrupts the second speaker, saying merrily: "Gentlemen, it doesn't really matter in which language you honor me in because I am deaf!" After a while, he interrupts the speaker again and begins to give his own speech. He points out that a lot can be learned about a culture from looking at their bathrooms and toilets.

The overly ceremonious atmosphere gives way to natural, good-natured merriment. Later, we are served tea. Sitting beside Loos is his friend, General Klecanda. A great number of prominent people have come to celebrate Loos.

The evening is spent at Dr. Müller's in the villa Loos built. Loos conducts the conversation. The guests assemble in the large main room, then proceed into the dining room. How wonderful the marble table looks with the round mahogany tabletop. At Loos' express wish, no tablecloth has been laid out, only little mats. He says:

"The most elegant tablecloth is a beautiful tabletop!"

After dinner some of the guests retire into the women's drawing room and some into the men's drawing room; both rooms are nice and cozy.

Karl Kraus, the unapproachable, is telling amusing anecdotes. Machar reports about Masaryk, to whose home he was invited for lunch.

The evening is charming and jovial... it is hard to leave such wonderful hosts.

On the occasion of his sixtieth birthday, Loos received,

in addition to his yearly pension, an honorarium from the Czechoslovak Department of Education for his outstanding artistic achievements.

AT THE PARK HOTEL

We are in Vienna again! This time we have taken a room at the Park Hotel out in Hietzing. Life here is pleasant and nice. Kulka drops by in the mornings to discuss business matters. The Kuhner house is currently under construction. Guests come over for tea in the afternoons. Kiki, a sweet little Japanese dog, enjoys the surroundings too. Unfortunately, Kiki has not been house-trained yet.

"You are going to have to get her into the habit of going out on the balcony," says Loos gently.

Kiki gets locked out on the balcony for hours on end. This method works. Kiki is house-trained. But, miracle of miracles, there aren't any spots that are even slightly damp out on the balcony either! The mystery soon finds an explanation. One evening, just as the dance music is beginning to float up into our rooms, the waiter from downstairs bursts in:

"Madame," he says loudly, gasping for breath, "there is terrible agitation downstairs, it has – has been raining on our best tables! I tried to calm down the guests by saying that Madame was probably watering her flowers, but since they couldn't see any flowers, they didn't believe it and got very upset!"

During the course of this somewhat bewildering

conversation we have both gone out to the terrace, here we find Kiki pressing her body up against the railing, barking happily at me because she undoubtedly thinks I approve of her good idea!

The waiters continue being friendly to us, despite this rather embarrassing incident, because they all love Kiki! And she is quite a clever little character. The instant she senses someone watching her, she immediately starts to flirt and do the craziest tricks; if no one pays any attention to her, she pouts and gets angry. Loos loves her. There are often jealousy scenes between this cunning little lady dog and me. I decide that our next dog will be a male, totally disregarding the fact that Kiki is still in the best of health and there is no reason to give her away.

Loos has discovered a young painter.

He commissions a picture from him, which, says Loos, will in fact have to be painted on a wall. It will be for Herr B.'s dining room. Herr B. has the misfortune to live exactly opposite a factory. It is a depressing view, particularly from the dining room. Loos puts up sheer golden yellow curtains at the windows which, when drawn, drench the room in sunlight. On the wall opposite the windows, he leaves a large part open in the light wood paneling. Here on the wall, which beforehand must be carefully prepared with egg whites, the young painter Aigner paints his picture. It shows three strong figures, peasants, navigating a small boat. A few pieces of driftwood stick up out of the water. The picture is simple but is interesting in its composition and spatial distribution. Loos likes its simplicity. Still, he is not entirely satisfied. "This picture has to be so impressive," says Loos, "that the poor man who lives here forgets that he has an ugly factory right in front of his nose and thinks that this picture is the view from his window. It must seem to be that close. That fresh and vibrant in its colours. This is only possible if it is painted directly on the wall, without a frame, without glass. We are approaching an era when frescoes will become modern again." There are still a few things in the design of the picture that he does not find quite right. He has them changed. "You must go to Paris, young man," he repeats again and again, "an artist suffocates here in Vienna!"

THE ELECTIONS

When the elections were being held in Austria four years ago and Loos was asked whom he would vote for – Loos is Czechoslovak – he answered: "Starhemberg."

"But your ideas are more in line with the Social Democrats!" Loos nods.

" And you would still vote for Starhemberg?"

Loos: "Yes, because I think Starhemberg is a capable human being."

" And if you could determine the ballot list by yourself?"

"Karl Kraus."

LAPIS LAZULI

We are at a small spa again taking the waters. We are staying at the best hotel – but in the worst room! Kiki, the dog, Loos and I. Kiki loves it and constantly wants to go for rides in a hackney-carriage. She always has to sit beside the coachman and be the center of attention. But if you dare not look at her, she will bark like crazy. Otherwise, she sits quietly, proud, unapproachable.

We have run low on money, I am in a bad mood, Loos is bored, he also does not like the taste of the water from the spring! One day Loos comes home very distressed.

"I met Doctor X., can you imagine, Lerle, he lent me 250 dollars 25 years ago and now he wants to have the money back. What do you think about that, Lerle?" Loos is outraged. I say nothing. I sigh and contemplate our predicament. Pay up or leave. Maybe the dear man will forget about it and we will not meet again for another 25 years.

Then Frau W. bursts into the room. She is a charming young woman, an ardent admirer of Loos. "Loos," she rejoices, "I have a wonderful piece of news for you! Dr. X. would like you to remodel his hotel."

"Is that the same Dr. X.?"

"One and the same."

"Didn't he tell you anything about his project?"

Loos nods anxiously. "Well, yes he did, but I will not be able to work for him; I know we will not get along!"

"Why not, Dolfi?"

Loos sulkily shrugs his shoulders.

"But Dolfi, you could earn a lot of money, the debt could be deducted from that, and we could use the rest to take a trip to France!"

Loos is still upset. Money doesn't interest him, but he would like to take a trip to France. "Alright then," he says finally, "I will take the job, but I will tell you one thing, Lerle, if Dr. X. ever tries to force me to do something I do not want to, we are leaving immediately, Lerle!"

I promise that we will.

The first meeting goes fairly well. Herr Dr. X. kills me with his fierce looks, he threatens me that I will have to pay for a lost season if the construction is not completed on time, but otherwise everything goes quite smoothly.

Loos inspects the building. As usual, the basic plan is drawn up within five minutes, here an opening will be made, there a wall removed, from these two dark chambers one large room constructed, and so on. Dr. X. nods with enthusiasm. He is swept along by the tempo, by the quick practical thinking of this man, mesmerized. He is a very intelligent man and I cannot understand my husband's misgivings!

Dr. X. invites us for tea at his apartment. The sitting room is furnished in dark mahogany and the walls, too, are paneled in mahogany, the curtains are dark. "Here, this is my favorite room," says Dr. X. contentedly. "I know, Loos, that this room is in keeping with your style."

"With my style? Dear doctor, this is not a living room, this is a crypt!" Icy silence. The master of the house, peeved, lights himself a cigarette and says defiantly:

"I cannot stand those modern colourful things," then, resuming, "You do work a lot with mahogany, with dark subdued colours..."

Loos shakes his head. "Since my stay in Paris, that has fundamentally changed. I love bright colours. My most recent and most favorite dining room is quite colourful. Green, black, red, silver, highly polished – cheap softwoods! My best work!"

Dr. X anxiously: "Well, I would still prefer dark subdued colours in my building. Preferably mahogany."

Loos has lost himself in reverie for a few seconds and is not paying attention. Suddenly: "I have a splendid idea for you, Herr Doctor! We will panel the lobby in blue lapis lazuli. Blue lapis lazuli, it will look fabulous!"

Shocked, the doctor drops the cigarette from his hand. "Lapis lazuli? Are you crazy. Loos? That is way too expensive, I am not a millionaire!"

Loos: "It is no more expensive than good marble." (As a matter of fact, once Loos received a brochure; it said it is now possible to cut lapis lazuli extremely thin and to mount it onto plaster of Paris so that it can be used as a wall covering and still not be overly expensive.) Loos undeterred: "It will look fabulous. The Blue Grotto looks like nothing compared to this!"

The doctor angrily: "I would not think of it!"

Loos fantasizing: "People will be streaming here from all over the world just to see this wonder! You will attract a tremendous number of people, Herr Doctor!"

Doctor X. furiously: "I wouldn't think of it, even it were cheaper than paper! I wouldn't think of it! People would think I was very rich and I would have to pay even more taxes. And as soon as they saw the lobby, the guests would not dare ask the price, they would run out. Out of the question, Herr Loos! I will not use any lapis lazuli! It should look simple and comfortable here. I wouldn't think of it!"

Loos calmly: "You are being stupid, doctor, believe me! You will often think back to my words! You do not know what is good and beautiful!" Sarcastically: "I suppose you would prefer that I decorate everything in a rustic peasant style, like the parlor in an old German farmhouse with hearts painted on the wall, that would really be cozy! By the way, you would fit in there very well, Herr Doctor!"

The doctor, snow white: "What am I? I would fit into a farmhouse parlor? I'm going to get another architect!... I was counting you as one of my friends, but that is really going too far!" He opens the door, I want to say something else, boom, the door is slammed shut behind us.

"Dolfi!"

"I said at the very beginning, Lerle, that I cannot work with that man! Why did you talk me into doing it! Now you see what happens when you don't go along with me!"

We walk, unhappy, back to the hotel. Sighing, I pack, and get everything ready. Loos has lain down on the bed with Kiki lying on his chest. Frau W. comes in. The poor woman pales as she finds out everything. She feels very awkward about the whole story. She is friends with Dr. X... she admires Loos very much. Perplexed, she remains sitting a few minutes. Then a shimmer of hope spreads over her pretty face.

"Please don't leave yet," she says, "I will talk to Dr. X." Three hours later, she comes back out of breath. She is very pale, about to collapse from exhaustion. "I have spoken to Dr. X., it was not easy. In the beginning, he didn't want to hear a single word and almost kicked me out the door. But finally, because he does basically like Loos too, he settled down! He is sorry for having caused such a scene... after all, Dr. X. did find the remodelling plans completely to his liking... The interior decorating is a different matter however! Being an artist, Loos sometimes simply has ideas that a simple man cannot go along with."

Loos, the artist, is now in bed. This time he is really deaf. No, he does not want anything more to do with this man. Now only the threat that he really will have to pay back the 250 dollars and go to Pilsen instead of Paris moves him to take up negotiations again.

The lapis lazuli is not mentioned again! But at night, before falling asleep, he murmurs to himself, "Lapis lazuli... lapis lazuli... lapis lazuli..."

LOOS' IDEA FOR RENEWING THE BONDS OF THE FRENCH-CZECHOSLOVAK ALLIANCE

We learn that the writer Marcel Ray is staying in Prague, accompanied by a French minister. It is impossible for Loos to leave B. to go and see Marcel Ray. He decides to send me immediately on a mission to Prague.

"As soon as you arrive," says Loos, "you are to go to the French embassy in Hradschin. You will present your calling card and ask that they admit you first, ahead of everyone else. You are to tell Marcel Ray the following:

"First: I, Adolf Loos, would like to found a school of architecture in Paris. I need funds for this school that I do not have. Ask if the French government would like to do something for me.

"Second: I visited Versailles last year. The palace is still in good condition, but the stone pavement in the courtyard in front of the palace has completely deteriorated. Tell Marcel Ray I have the following idea: Czechoslovakia has the cheapest paving stones and an excellent knowledge of how to work with them. I have never seen paving anywhere in the world as beautiful and as original as in Prague. Since people usually do not look up when they are walking but instead down on the ground, an attractive pavement has nowadays almost become more important than the facades of the houses. The French should commission some Czechoslovak pavers to go to Versailles. They should incorporate the French and the Czechoslovak crests into the pavement to commemorate and strengthen the French-Czechoslovak Alliance. It certainly would be a great honor for Czechoslovakia to present France this paving as a gift.

"Then tell Marcel Ray that he and the minister should go and look at the house I built in Prague. Understood? Repeat it! Good!... Your train leaves in half an hour."

"Right now?"

"Yes, immediately! Take Kiki along so that you do not feel so lonely."

So Kiki and I travel all night long. In the early morning, the receptionist at the embassy in Hradshin is hardly delighted when a sleepy woman in a gray travelling dress, a dog on her arm, knocks on the door and demands to be let in immediately. Distrustful, he leads her into a white salon with furniture covered in light blue damask. Here she waits many, many hours. Kiki, the dog, has conjured up a large dark stain on the beautiful sofa... Morning sun breaks through the high windows, painting gray frames on the golden, reflective floor. A servant in a red coat with gold trim finally comes in. The double doors open: Marcel Ray.

In a friendly manner he shakes my hand, asks how his friend Loos is doing. He is a man with intelligent, clear features. I make my request. He listens to me smiling, then says:

"To found a Loos School would be an achievement for the youth of today. I will do my very best to see that it will be brought to life. The idea of paving the courtyard at Versailles is original and I like it very much. I will suggest it... To see the house by Loos is my greatest wish. I will go there as soon as possible... Thank you very much!"

That very same day Marcel Ray went with the French minister to the Müller house that Loos built in Prague.

THE MILL RESTAURANT

Loos has a new idea. He wants to turn a small mill near Prague into a place for excursions and a restaurant. Near Paris there are several very elegant places of this kind.

While the guests listen to the cheerful clapping of the mill, champagne is being drunk diligently. Anyone can watch in the kitchen how the joint is being roasted on a spit over a large open fire.

Loos discovers a small mill near Prague, which seems suitable to him. He gets a developer, Dr. Kapsa, interested in the idea, who drives out with us, accompanied by his wife, to inspect the mill.

Loos wants to start out small. The grassy plot in front of the house on the waterfront should be tidied up, a few tables with colourful tablecloths set out. The large courtyard is well suited to park the cars, a dining room for guests can be arranged for rainy weather. The miller is a simple man who is quite willing to provide the place at a low rent.

On the other side of the grass, by the water, is a small overgrown garden. "Here," says Loos, "there will be a little menagerie. A couple of monkeys, exotic birds, and when more money is available, a few more animals will be added."

A wine merchant in Prague is then sought out to supply beverages.

The whole plan falls through in the end though because the road from Prague to the small mill is too difficult for cars. The money to have the road fixed, of course, cannot be found.

AND ALL THE BELLS SHOULD RING

Herr X. comes to us and says the wood paneling is too expensive, he would like to try and get it cheaper. "The carpenter," he says, "is overcharging me. I want to bargain him down."

Loos falls silent. Then he looks his client straight in the eye: "Let me tell you something," he says, "and may all the bells of the city ring this out: Never bargain a worker down! You should never pressure a craftsman into giving you a lower price, the only option left to him is to give you material of a lesser quality or to do sloppy work. Give him rather a little more money than he asks for and you will receive a thousand times better work, he will work with a lot more pleasure because he is being recognized..."

GENERAL K.'S CASTLE

We are sitting in a coffee house in a small town. An elegant, handsome officer comes rushing over to us. General K. "My dearest friend." He embraces Loos and beams with happiness. "Loos...!"

Dolfi introduces him: "General K. – my wife. See, Lerle, this is the man I have brought misfortune upon. When I was giving my lectures at the Sorbonne in Paris, he was my most assiduous student. I said once back then that the only reason the Germans lost the war was because they marched more slowly than the French. I also thought their laced up boots were not very practical. What did this man do? He returned back home and tried to introduce some innovative changes in the military system based on my ideas. So now they have transferred him to a small town!"

Loos makes an endearingly childlike, wistful face. "That is what happens to my students when they try to implement my ideas."

General K.: "But Loos, your lectures were my greatest experiences! I am proud to be called your student! I am only stationed here temporarily and will be going to L. soon. Why don't you come visit me there sometime? Besides, I would like to remodel my house."

This comment has aroused my business sense. I say: "I

am sure next week we will be going to L."

Loos has for some time buried himself in a pile of newspapers. The words "structural changes" have not made the slightest impression on him. After General K. has left, I say; "Dolfi, General K. has a palace, this will make a terrific project for you!" But Loos is reading, he is not receptive at the moment.

A week later, we are having tea at General K.'s. A small group of aristocrats has also been invited. The old structure is simply beautiful! Gobelin tapestries hang on the walls, few, but authentic old pieces of furniture are sensibly placed throughout the room. One's gaze, however, is captured by the magnificent view. Through the giant window one sees blooming trees and the city, dream-like in the light of the setting sun.

Loos cannot tear himself away from the view. The wife of General K. pulls him aside.

"Dear Loos, we would like to remodel this old house and put in modern furnishings."

Loos pales in anger. "Remodel?... You want to remodel this magnificent house?... Put in modern furnishings?... You want to distract the eye from this magnificent view to the interior furnishings, to marble walls and beautiful wood? Don't you see that the very lack of decoration, the profound simplicity of these walls reinforces the impression a hundred times?"

The wife of the general wants to respond.

"Don't touch it!" With that, Loos cuts short any debate. The matter is settled.

We soon leave. At home, I cannot resist saying something. "Dolfi, what you said is all well and good, but there are other rooms besides the great hall that can be altered. I believe Frau K. also wanted a more convenient staircase. People come from all over the world to visit there and would then have seen your rooms."

Loos is sitting buried in a fortress of newspapers. He looks at me annoyed. "If someone wants to find me, he will find me," he says.

LA BOUTIQUE D'ADOLF LOOS

We want to start a business. It will be called "La Boutique d'Adolf Loos." Loos has the following idea: He wants to begin producing a fairly large series of a particular style of stool. Since the stools would be mass-produced, the purchase price would be low. Once a certain amount of the stools has been sold, another object will be mass-produced, like the sugar shaker that Loos found in Paris and which he finds particularly practical and pretty. The pieces left over from each series would be sold later in the actual boutique.

Unfortunately, it turns out that even with mass production such high-quality objects would be too expensive.

I still want to apply for a patent on the stools, which are very original. Loos laughs at me. The model was found in an Egyptian royal tomb.

LOOS AND THE JEWS

Loos said: "The Jews have brought anti-Semitism on themselves by saying: We are the chosen people!"

Loos wants to be best man at the Jewish wedding of a young student. This is not permitted by the Jewish religion, since he is a Catholic. Loos shakes his head in bewilderment. A Jew can be best man at a Christian wedding. Why is it that a Christian cannot be best man at a Jewish wedding?

He said to me once: "I am an anti-Semite. All Christians should marry Jewish women and vice-versa. In 400 years there won't be any more Jews... I already have my second Jewish wife..."

Many students of Loos, students who have worked with him for years, are Jews. Loos says: "I would like to have more Christians among my students, if possible a few aristocrats. Aristocrats are born with culture, they would have to be good architects! But when they become poor, they strangely enough become chauffeurs!"

THE DEPARTURE

Loos is itching to take a trip; it is impossible to hold him back. He has to go, just simply has to go! My mother, who is forever mothering, is very worried.

"You will catch your death," she says, because he has a bit of a cold.

"Oh, mother," Loos replies, "That does not matter! Just imagine I were to die here! No, I would not want to cause you such trouble, I rather leave."

Suddenly I am not feeling very well. I go to bed with fever. Loos most lovingly tends to me for two days. As soon as the fever has subsided, he declares:

"Get up, we are leaving at noon!"

My mother expresses new misgivings.

"Alright then," says Loos, "She can stay home – I am leaving!"

"By yourself?" asks mother.

"Oh," says Loos, "at the most, I will take another woman along with me!"

We leave for the station at noon. Loos is beaming, he has gotten his way.

Nürnberg: Dined at the Bratwurstglöckle in the evening... spent half the night strolling through the medieval city!

Frankfurt: Loos visits the wife of Professor Klimt and Professor Baumeister! He takes me to the Jewish quarter, has the temple caretaker show him the old house of the Rothschild's! We tour the new housing developments! Loos really likes these developments. "They are very well constructed... they could be mine," says Loos.

Mannheim: Platz, the city architect, takes us on a tour through the city. He shows us the Goethe Theater, which Loos particularly likes. He regrets that there is so little time to spend with Loos in Mannheim. A man who knows what he wants, a man who knows who Loos is...!

Heidelberg: "I did not know Heidelberg before," says Loos, "I am so happy to get to know it!"

We stroll along the river, walk up to the castle and dine there in a very beautiful hotel. The spring sun is warm and pleasant. "I would like to come here again during my lifetime," says Loos.

Darmstadt: Loos goes to see a furniture manufacturer the same evening we arrive. He regrets not being able to meet with him. First thing the next morning, before I am up, he goes to the chair factory and orders a few excellent pieces for Czechoslovakia. Before we leave, he takes me to visit the so-called artist colony. The house of Behrens – the necktie pattern artist, as Loos refers to him – brings an amused smile to Loos' lips.

"There are people already today who are laughing with me about these artist colonies... A few years ago, I was the only one! But it will not take long..."

We travel to Stuttgart. A Loos exhibition, lots of pictures, a few wooden models are being shown here in the commercial arts school! Schleicher, a building commissioner and one of Loos' former students, is waiting for us at the station. He is as excited as a child to see Loos again. We settle down in a hotel. First thing the next morning we go to the exhibition. Loos begins to talk while standing in front of a picture from the Kuhner house. He pulls a matchbox out of his pocket:

"You see," he says loudly, "this is modern architecture! The houses of the future will not be constructed out of steel supported concrete that you have to blow up with ecrasite in order to get rid of them – as was the case at the last exhibition in Paris,... the house of the future is made of wood! Like the little Japanese houses! It has moveable walls! Modern architecture is: Japanese culture plus European tradition!"

A crowd of people has congregated around Loos. More and more people are coming in from the other rooms. Loos becomes more and more animated... the fire of youth shines in his eyes! Later, he tells me:

"It is impossible for me to give a great speech in front of a single person. The more people are listening to me, the more intense the atmosphere is, the easier it becomes for me to speak. I have never prepared for a speech! Whatever I say is always improvised on the spot. It would be impossible for me to read a speech off a piece of paper!"

Later that very same day, I have to write an express letter to Mitzi: "Dear Mitzi, please send to us here immediately the black drinking glasses that Josef Hoffmann designed."

"What do you want to do with the drinking glasses from Josef Hoffmann?"

Dolf gets a mischievous look on his face. "I want to give them to the Museum of Tasteless Objects, which is here in Stuttgart, there they will fit right in!"

We travel on to Zürich.

MILAN

A former student of Loos' is expecting us in Milan: De Finetti. But it is someone else who is really responsible for Loos coming here. Elsie Altmann, the charming Viennese dancer and former wife of Loos. That very same evening we go with De Finetti to the theater where she is dancing. Loos asks me to find Elsie backstage and ask her to spend the evening with us after the performance.

She comes, wearing a simple black dress and a black patent leather feather hat that looks wonderful on her.

"How lovely you look, Elsie," Loos says tenderly. "And you are still young and slender. Are you happy?"

Elsie takes a pencil and writes, "I am alone. I have nothing else in the world but my big suitcase. I travel with it all over the wide, wide, world..."

Dolf's mouth twitches as he reads those words. Then he takes her hand and kisses it. A tear falls on it...

De Finetti lives with his young wife in a large beautiful apartment house that belongs to his family. The apartment reminds me of home. It is a real Loos apartment. Loos walks through the rooms and nods, satisfied. The floor in the dining room is made of small red tiles. It looks very attractive. Loos studies it carefully. "These decorative tiles keep the room cool," explains De Finetti.

Loos decides to use the same floor in a house that he is supposed to build in Palestine. He is not ashamed to also learn something from his students.

NICE

We have reached Nice, the city of dreams. Loos is as happy as a little boy.

"Lerle," he calls out, "let's go for a ride in a cab and I will show you the city."

"Shouldn't we go to a hotel first?" I say, enviously watching the other travellers who, with their towers of luggage, are instructing chauffeurs to take them to their destination. "I am tired."

"No. The luggage can stay here at the station, we will go and look for accommodation. I am not going to check in at the first best hotel! I am going to prove to you that Nice is not only the most beautiful, but also the cheapest city in the world..."

We drive through the city. The red houses on the Place de la Concorde seem strange to me. I do not like the old casino on the waterfront at all.

Loos laughs. "The Hotel Babylon that I am going to build here on the Promenade des Anglais will definitely be more to your liking!"

"But Dolfi, there is not any space on the Promenade des Anglais!"

"Oh, these houses will simply be torn down."

Looking somewhat closer, I do indeed see a sign on

almost every house: "For Sale."

"First thing tomorrow, I want you to go to the real estate agent and get some price quotes. We must not waste any time, we have to be well-prepared for when we find a wealthy financier."

Loos orders the carriage to stop at the Hotel Ruhl. Ten bellboys rush towards me to help me out of the carriage.

"See, it is a good thing we do not have our luggage along," says Loos, "these lads would have carried it in a long time ago."

I get out. "A room, Madame? 100 francs par jour."

"Get back in," says Loos, "that is way too expensive."

We drive on. At the next hotel the same scenario repeats itself, a room here costs 80 francs.

"Keep going," says Loos. "Keep going, keep going!"

Time passes, we have been driving around for two hours now. Loos is getting fresher and livelier by the minute. I, on the other hand, am tired. Astonished, Loos has the driver stop.

"Tired, Lerle? Driver, do you perhaps happen to know a good, cheap hotel?"

"Oui, Monsieur!"

It is not exactly by the beach.... No bellboys in colourful uniforms run over to us. A fat man, ruddy complexion, in a white apron, bows deeply in front of us: the "patron." We both climb out. The owner himself proudly takes us to a bright, white room. There is a red carpet on the floor and running water. "And the price?"

"35 francs par jour with full pension, Monsieur!"

Loos beams. "We will stay here. Neither in Vienna nor in Prague will you find such a nice, cheap, little hotel – with running water!"

LOOS REBUILDS THE RIVIERA

The days pass in unceasing work. Loos has contacted all the real estate agents who deal with the selling of houses and property. The news that a famous architect wants to buy some land spreads like wildfire among them. Every day friendly agents show up unsolicited and offer property and houses. All of Nice can be had for a cheap price.

"Don't you think, Dolfi, that this cheap hotel makes a bad impression?"

Loos looks at me astonished. "To the contrary, Lerle. Swindlers always live in expensive hotels... I am not a swindler..."

He never tires of looking over property with the agents. Calculations are made, measurements taken, bartering done. Dead tired, but healthy as never before, he returns at lunchtime. I dare once to softly ask a question:

"Dolfi, how can any of this end well? We do not have any money!"

He looks at me disappointed. Defiant, like a child who is about to have his favorite toy taken away, he replies: "How can you spoil the enjoyment I am getting from working on this project by asking that, Lerle! Didn't I tell you we have to be ready for when the rich financier shows up?!" Irritated, he leaves me; soon he has rebuilt the entire

Riviera in his head.

I sigh, but he fantasizes, builds and hopes... fantasizes and builds!

BEAU-BEAU

It is Sunday. The house brokers and property salesmen are not around today. We take a hackney-cab and go for a ride. We drive inland for a change. Soon the sea and the city are far behind us. With the wide-open eyes of a child, Loos looks at the blooming fields of wild poppies, the weathered old farmhouses, the peasants, dressed in black, walking towards us. A big ugly dog jumps up barking at our carriage and accompanies us a little way.

"You know," Loos says cheerily, "We should get a dog again."

I have been thinking the whole time that Loos will not give up his search for a dog. I had secretly hoped that he would, for I shudder at the thought of having to get up at five in the morning and all the other unpleasantness I had inherited with Kiki. But Loos is so happy today and in such a good mood that I do not want to spoil anything for him. "Yes, Dolfi, a dog... Maybe we can buy one in Nice."

"Driver," Loos calls out, "you wouldn't happen to know of a dog dealer who has little Japanese dogs?"

"Mais oui monsieur! I know a woman, it isn't at all far from here," he says, pointing with the end of the whip to a village on the horizon, "that is where her house is, monsieur. She has very beautiful dogs."

"Let's go," says Loos. "Driver," he calls concerned and makes him stop again. "Won't the horse get hungry? We have been underway several hours already!"

The driver sets his mind at ease. He has some feed along with him and will feed the horse at Madame Sou's.

We drive on. We are all in a wonderful mood. Loos, because he is looking forward to the dog, I, because Loos is in such a good mood, the driver, because we are going for such a long ride, the horse, because it will soon get something to eat... But Madame Sou's house is not at all that nearby, we drive on for at least an hour. We stop finally in front of a nice very small house with a large yard. Madame Sou is sitting outside in a flowered housecoat. She comes toward us, talking loudly. A number of dogs barking in all different tonalities accompany her. The dogs are very charming, but even she doubts that they are purebreds. She consoles us by saying that purebred dogs would be less intelligent than these ones here, which she is definitely not wrong about.

Loos is disappointed. He is playing with the little ones, but does not say a word about buying. A little blond girl comes out of the house. She curtsies to us. In her arms she is carrying a very small, long-haired, light brown dog. In the middle of his forehead is a white, triangular spot.

"Hand me your dog for a moment," Loos calls out briskly.

She does not really want to let go of him. Loos takes the little dog on his lap and scratches him gently. "He is not exactly purebred either," he comments, "his muzzle is too large and his legs are too long. But he definitely has something, this dog. Look, he has eyes like a human being! Do you like him, Lerle?"

I take him. He happily licks my cheeks and gently nuzzles up to me. No, this dog is not deceitful like Kiki, he will not betray me. I like him a lot. We buy Beau-Beau…

The little girl and her mother ride along with us for a whole stretch, and that comforts the child a little. We become friends with Madame Sou immediately. She gives us lots of good advice for Beau-Beau, which we will not follow. She wants to come visit us in Nice. We say good-bye. The little girl takes a large, checked handkerchief out of her pocket and waves as the carriage finally rolls on again.

Loos waves his gray hat. He is still waving it long after the two have disappeared behind the next crossing.

A FINANCIER APPEARS AND DISAPPEARS

It is the height of the tourist season. The entire city takes on a vibrant appearance. The Promenade des Anglais is packed with people. You see the same people here that you meet in Karlsbad, in Vienna on the Kärntnerstrasse and in St. Moritz.

Loos, lost in thought, stares at the sea, the dog and the people. A short, heavy-set man and a blond woman give us a friendly wave. Loos becomes lively. "Quick, Lerle, go and get him, this is the man I am looking for!"

I edge my way through the crowd. It is in vain, it seems the ground has swallowed the two of them. Loos is very agitated. "This man is one of the most enterprising people of our times. He would have understanding for my projects. He has the money, the connections, and the potential to build. I would also give him the good advice, which he will never regret, to build here and not in Berlin. Nice is still a city with a future for a lot of people... This man could understand me!"

"Dolfi, who is that man?"

"Herr von L. from Berlin."

Despite diligent searching we do not meet him again. He had been staying at the Hotel Ruhl. Loos writes him a letter; the reply comes from Rome. Herr von L. has received the letter. He finds the projects very interesting, but it does not seem to him profitable enough to build in Nice. Otherwise he would be happy to be of service. Loos disappointed puts the letter aside.

September 1934. I am sitting with Herr von L., who is now in the business of buying European factories for China, in the foyer of the Hotel Alcron in Prague. We chat.

"I never was a great fan of Loos," he says resolutely, "but he was right back then with his idea of building in Nice instead of in Berlin."

VISIT TO A CEMETERY

The cemetery of Nice is situated high above the city. We drive up the hill on the gentle road. The sky is a deep blue, the sea a deep blue. Loos was not exaggerating. I have never seen such beautiful grounds. The graves are not crowded close together, there are no high walls to obstruct the view. The tombstones stand, bright and peaceful, in the sun – the hill has a gentle slope – they overlook the sea.

Loos walks seriously and slowly down the wide gravel path and looks thoughtfully at the gravestones and inscriptions. He remains standing in front of one grave for a long time. On the stone is written: "God picked an unopened rosebud. In His mercy he wanted to spare her the suffering of life. F.L., eighteen years of age." Loos raises his arms: "If I die in Nice, I would like to be buried here. There is such a beautiful view of the sea from here!"

I have become impatient by now. Annoyed, I pull on his coat. "Dolfi, come, the driver has been waiting so long already. Come on now!"

But he does not leave just yet. "Promise me, Lerle, that I will not be cremated when I die. A dead body is fertile humus. Nothing in the world should be wasted..."

DEPARTURE FROM NICE

One day, Madame Sou actually does come to visit us. Over her pinned up curls she is wearing a large black straw hat with floppy cornflowers on it. Madame Sou finds that Beau-Beau is not in the best shape and that he is very nervous.

"You are not feeding him meat by any chance, are you?" she asks suspiciously.

Loos nods. "But of course!"

"Oh, monsieur," Madame Sou moans, "he is too small, he needs to eat rice, not meat!"

But Loos pounds excitedly on the table. "Madame," he says, "Count Thun in Vienna, who is a first-class specialist in animal care, always gives his dogs meat. A dog is a carnivorous animal. Wild dogs eat only meat."

Madame Sou, who doesn't know who Count Thun in Vienna is, moans unhappily. "Beau-Beau is not a wild dog," she says, "poor little Beau-Beau!" She leaves soon afterwards. She gives us one more piece of advice, which we do follow. Beau-Beau should not be taken along to all the coffee houses, it will not do him any harm if he stays home sometimes and sleeps.

And so we leave him at home and go out to a coffee house. We take a stroll, it gets late. It is after nine o'clock when we come home. The hotel owner is waiting for us in front of the hotel. His red face is even redder than usual. He rushes towards me without greeting us.

"You must leave our hotel, Madame! I have been to your room. Oh, you did not tell me you had a dog! Oh, you are not allowed to have dogs here... My entire, beautiful room, ruined!"

"What happened?" asks Loos. "Why is the owner so red in the face?"

We have to move out because of Beau-Beau," I reply, "dogs are not allowed here."

"Sir, you dare to insult my dog?! It does not say anywhere that dogs are not allowed here! Why do you only tell us that now?! You do not know at all how to appreciate a guest like me! See here, it is written in all the French newspapers that I am staying at your hotel," and he hands the astonished owner a newspaper that does indeed say: "Adolf Loos in Nice, staying at Hotel N." "No one has ever given you such advertising!"

With that, Loos grabs me and we majestically climb the stairs. In our room there is wild chaos. On the floor are some neat little piles and damp spots. The turned-down bedcovers have been pulled onto the floor, dirty and torn. In the middle of this wildness, lies Beau-Beau, the offender, asleep.

Dolfi whispers to me: "Lerle, Lerle, the owner was right. For 35 francs a day with full board one really can't be allowed to do something like this. There is nothing left to salvage. Pack, we are leaving immediately. Give a princely tip!"

An hour later, we are sitting together with the offender in the car. We drive to the best, most beautiful, most expensive hotel on the Riviera, the Hotel Cap d'Antibes on the Cap d'Antibes.

ARRIVAL AT THE HOTEL CAP D'ANTIBES

The arrival at the Hotel Cap d'Antibes is like a fairy tale. Uniformed servants await the approaching car. Our luggage is swiftly unloaded. Like some long-awaited royal couple we stride though the foyer. Left and right the personnel bow deeply. Behind us, his tail held high, marches Beau-Beau, the dog. Everything is festively lit up...

"A room with a bath please!" As Loos writes his name, the doorman gives a start and then bows deeply.

"What an honor!" he says melodiously, "the great architect from Vienna." The owner walks toward us with open arms. He himself takes us to our suite.

"We have a dog along; that is permitted here, isn't it?"

"But of course," says the owner loudly. With lively gestures, he assures us what a pleasure the presence of Beau-Beau gives him.

"See, Beau-Beau," Loos says, beaming, "this is the right hotel for you!"

The door closes. We are alone.

"It is beautiful here!" I whisper.

Loos cheerfully rubs his hands together. "See, Lerle, didn't I tell you from the start, life with a dog is quite something else? Without Beau-Beau we never would have come here!"

JOSEPH ROTH

We are sitting over a cup of black coffee after an opulent dinner. Suddenly, Loos points out to me a young man who is speaking energetically amid a group of Americans. He is slender, blond, and has his lightly wavy hair with a parting to the side. His face is very likable. Intelligent eyes, a slender, curved nose, a fine and somewhat melancholic mouth.

"That is Joseph Roth, Lerle. Go over and tell him I would like to meet him."

I really hate it when he gives me such orders. But Loos is opposed to any kind of superfluous social convention. He would talk to the man himself, but his deafness prevents him from doing that. I get up. I desperately glance around, trying to find a waiter who could do the task for me, but, like in any large hotel, there is never one there when you need him. I take advantage of an opportunity to speak to Joseph Roth as he goes to fetch an ashtray from a table nearby. My shyness immediately turns into arrogance.

"Herr Roth," I say, "Adolf Loos, whose name I am sure you are familiar with, would like to meet you."

Joseph Roth looks at me astonished and amused. "Adolf Loos? Is he here? Of course I know him, indeed, I know him personally, from Paris."

As he notices my embarrassment, he then adds, smiling: "Of course there were so many other people there... he has probably forgotten about it."

Joseph Roth comes over to our table. We are sitting in the bright, light room of the hotel that looks so much like a castle. The double doors opening out to the sun-drenched terrace are wide open. Steps lead down to the broad, blinding-white gravel path, which, sharply dividing the lawn into two deep green parts, drops straight to the sea. Water and sky blend, blue in blue.

"Are you working right now?" asks Loos.

Joseph Roth nods. "I am writing a new novel, 'Radetzky March', that takes place in pre-war Vienna."

"Are you going to be staying here very much longer?"

"I do not know exactly. I always have to be in the right surroundings for my work. As soon as my novel is finished, I'll be leaving from here."

Suddenly, I realize what the castle and the scenery here remind me of. The emperor's palace in Vienna, Schönbrunn.

I see Joseph Roth again. We have tea together. Joseph Roth looks at me contemplatively and says:

"Forgive me for the indiscrete question. But isn't it hard for you to live with a man who is so much older than you and deaf?"

It is strange, I am asked this question so often. As if other, younger, men do not have quite different flaws! I answer, patiently and truthfully:

"No, it is not difficult, because everything that I am, that I know and that I can do, I have learned from Loos. It has been said, that Loos has always had pretty wives. It is my opinion that the women became more beautiful by being with Loos and because of Loos. I am very happy!"

Joseph Roth looks at me smiling and remains silent.

REMARQUE

Whenever we arrive at a new place, at a new hotel, Loos is always sure to be given the guest book. We are sitting in the dining room, our dinner is finished, Loos is leafing through the guest book. He reads, turns a few more pages, gently shakes his head and says:

"No Czechoslovaks have ever stayed here except for us. Nothing but Englishmen, Americans, a few Frenchmen and Germans. Remarque, the writer, is also staying here. Garçon," he calls, "do you know the writer, Remarque?"

"Mais oui, monsieur, he is sitting over there with his wife."

It is hard to know what to do. Seated at the table in the corner are three gentlemen and a lady. Loos carefully eyes the group.

"Lerle," he says merrily, "make a guess! Which of the three, in your opinion, is Remarque?"

I think about it for a moment. "That is the one!" I point to a blond man with a high forehead and a sharp, bold nose, who is speaking animatedly with Frau Remarque. And then, somewhat uncertain: "Or do you think it is the pale one with the dark artistic curls, gazing dreamily into his compote?" The third man does not seem a likely candidate to me. His hair is dark blond, combed straight back, his face slender and very young, an average-looking face. His voice, however, sounds clear and to the point. I cannot understand any words.

"Well, Lerle?" I shrug my shoulders helplessly. The blond with the hooked nose or the brunette? I do not know.

Loos disappointed shakes his head. "Artistic curls, velvet collars and an animated bearing have nothing to do with art. Only artists that are not really artists resort to such gimmicks. That modest young man there with the clear youthful face will be Remarque." And so it was!

DEPARTURE FROM CAP D'ANTIBES

The Hotel Cap d'Antibes is starting to empty. Joseph Roth has left, Remarque too, and most of the Americans and Dutch. Only a few French, whom we do not know, remain. Some of the locals do come for afternoon teas in the charming pavilion down by the beach... but Loos is bored. Even the wonderful pool at the base of the red cliffs that belongs to the hotel cannot cheer him up. He needs work and people around him. We are told that Bernhard Shaw, who often spends time here in the summer, will undoubtedly be arriving soon. But Loos does not feel like waiting, he needs a change, he wants to leave.

Then something happens that postpones our departure: The owner of the hotel wants to remodel the hotel and asks Loos to make a plan for him. Loos does not think about leaving anymore. He excitedly paces off the property early in the morning. He writes a letter to Kurt Unger, his student, and asks him to come to us. There are long discussions with the owner of the hotel.

Loos, who likes the site of the hotel, does not want to change its castle-like character. He wants to make an addition on the left and right so that the guests do not have to dine down in the pavilion as was often the case up to now when there were lots of guests present. He wants to enlarge the foyer. Suddenly he is again lively and young, which he has not been in a long time.

But some family incident – I believe the brother of the hotel owner had passed away – takes him away from this construction project. All at once he declares that he does not want to build right now. He asks Loos for an invoice, which Loos indignantly refuses. He does not want money, he wants to build. The owner decides then to reduce our hotel bill to the minimum. This gesture puts Loos in a better mood again. He thanks him, exclaiming over and over again that he has never been to a more beautiful hotel with such a distinguished, select clientele as he found here. Still, he cannot be talked into staying.

We leave. We do not go far. The car takes us that same evening over a winding road, which stretches before us like a shining silver band along the water, to Juan les Pins.

Sequel: A few days later, we are lying, as usual, in lounge chairs on the beach. A young man, pale and tired, is moving slowly from chair to chair, from table to table.

Finally, he walks quickly toward us, breathing a sigh of relief. It is Kurt Unger, whom we had long since forgotten about.

"And how did you actually find us?" asks Loos, curious, after he has ordered the poor lad something to drink, after all we had not left our new address behind anywhere.

"I went back again to Nice from the Hotel Cap d'Antibes. In a restroom there, I saw a notice in a newspaper that read: 'Adolf Loos staying at Hotel N. in Nice.' But no one could give me any information at the Hotel N. either. The owner was not very nice to me at all."

"I can believe that," laughs Loos. "And how did you manage to find your way here?"

"Yes, well," says Kurt Unger, "I thought to myself, Juan les Pins is the only place where anything is happening right now. The other Riviera towns are almost empty. So I came here, hoping that I would find you."

"Bravo!" calls out Loos. "You are a thinking man. Bravo! You will make an excellent architect. Because a good architect must, above all, be able to think logically. You have to stay with us. Besides, it won't hurt you to learn to eat bouillabaisse. It's only fitting."

THE PINE TREES

We are strolling through Juan les Pins. "Where are the pine trees, les pins?" asks Loos, continuing along the coast. We walk through the little town. "Where are the pines?" complains Loos.

We stop a local man. "Tell me," Loos asks the Frenchman, "where are the pine trees of Juan les Pins?"

"Well," says the Frenchman, helplessly shrugging his shoulders, "a couple of years ago there was a whole pine tree forest here, but then they discovered the beach – the whole coast is rocky. They started building. The village got more visitors, hotels were needed, the trees were cut down, the land divided into lots, houses built."

"That's a pity," says Loos. "What a pity! One could have built and still spared the trees. That's a pity, really a pity!" He sadly looks at the ugly row of houses for which the trees had to be sacrificed.

"But now Juan les Pins is the most visited place around here," says the Frenchman, "money is coming in, and that's the main thing!"

I do not translate those words for my husband, because I am afraid of a burst of fury.

A few days later, Loos discovers a piece of property on which several magnificent pine trees are standing. Loos sends Kurt Unger out to find out what is supposed to happen with this piece of land. Kurt Unger reports back that the owner has the intention of building a small apartment house here.

Loos buys a drafting board and a ruler and is very busy for eight days. He drafts a plan. He works feverishly. "The pine tress, the pine trees," he exclaims over and over again, "must be saved!"

The project was immediately written up in a small article in a French newspaper. The house has a large round entrance gate which is so tall that the pine trees standing inside, in the middle of the courtyard, can be see from far away. The pine trees have been saved!

Loos is happy that he does not have to eat at one particular hotel but instead can go wherever he pleases. Everyday he comes back beaming:

"Lerle, today I have discovered another hotel, the daily special costs only 9 francs. Let's go there." Only coach drivers and locals eat there. We all get stomach upsets. But the next day, Loos comes back again with a new restaurant. He loves the Provençal earthenware, he loves the colourful tablecloths. He says:

"A time will come when everyone will be using earthenware. People will sit at bare tables or at ones covered with bright tablecloths, the restaurant owner in shirt-sleeves will write the price of the food in chalk on a blackboard. That is what the future restaurant business will look like. Cabbies and aristocrats will sit together at one table and everyone will be satisfied..." Every day an acquaintance or a stranger is brought over for lunch.

Loos tells amusing stories to entertain us. One of these true stories is the following. "Once, in Paris, I was assigned the task of guiding a group of foreigners, of the kind that show up in packs there. I took them to a genuine small French restaurant, where foreigners otherwise never go. The owner set a bowl of small fish on the table as hors d'oeuvres. 'What's this?' asks one. He fishes out, with his fingers wide apart, a fish, holds it up, then lets it glide vertically into his mouth. 'Na,' he said, 'that, I do not like.' The next one follows his example, also fishes out a small fish from the oil, slurps it up loudly and also says: 'Na, that doesn't taste good.' Everyone else in the group does the same. The bill comes. Surprise: everyone has to pay one franc for the hors d'oeuvres! It comes as quite a shock. They all have to pay the same, whether they ate one fish or ten. Somehow that does not want to sink in, worse than that, however, was the singing that the good old boys started up after dinner. And since a couple of Tyroleans were also there, a lot of yodeling went on. Shocked, the owner rushes over to Loos. 'Monsieur,' he asks, 'what kind of a wild bunch of people are these?' 'Wild bunch? These are my fellow countrymen, mein Herr... Austrians..."'

REJECTS

Loos receives a letter from the furniture store S. in Berlin. The owner, S., asks Loos to design a dining room for his exhibition in Cologne, to be built precisely according to his specifications and then exhibited there. Loos designs a dining room in black-red-green colours and incorporates softwoods and lacquer finishes, which give it a Japanese look.

Coffee and tea services and dinnerware are also to be shown at this exhibition. Loos designs some drinking glasses following the famous Napoleon pattern. He wants to send Provençal earthenware as dinnerware for the exhibit. Harder-working than ever, he visits new restaurants daily, and looks at the dishes. In a little-frequented restaurant, Loos finds some earthenware that pleases him very much. The next day is a holiday. Despite this, Loos drives to a little village near Cannes, where the manufacturer of the earthenware is supposed to be.

To regain strength, in Cannes we each drink a tiny glass of schnapps. Then we take a car and drive up into the mountains. The road is bumpy and takes us past flowering shrubs. High up is a little village. Here, earthenware is produced in every other house. Plates and clay jugs in bright colours are exhibited everywhere in the window displays. Loos rings the doorbell of a small, low-built house.

We are in luck, the owner is home. He takes us into a backroom where there is earthenware in all colours, huge Provençal water jugs and flower vases. Loos looks around. He takes a soup plate down from a shelf, looks it over carefully and sets it down in front of him.

The owner is very alarmed. "Excuse me, monsieur," he says, "but that is a reject!" Embarrassed, he grabs the plate away from Loos.

Loos looks at him and laughs. "This plate is especially beautiful. I would like twelve soup plates just like this one."

"But it was by accident that the brown colour ran into the yellow," says the proprietor in despair, "that definitely will not happen on those twelve plates!"

"This accident," says Loos, "is very pretty. It doesn't matter at all if the colour is not perfectly uniform. Make me twelve reject plates ... just like this one."

We go for a walk along the shore. Loos is wearing a funny-looking Japanese straw hat of the type now fashionable for ladies. A young, fifteen-year-old girl runs up to us:

"Oh, please, Mr. Chaplin, your autograph!"

Loos, who does not hear, takes the pen she offers and boldly writes "Adolf Loos."

The girl stands still a moment, surprised. "Then you are the great architect from Vienna?" And, after I nod: "That is terrific!"

"What did the little girl say?"

"She thought you were Chaplin."

Two days later is the gala showing of a Chaplin film. We share a private box with Countess T. Loos is wearing a dinner jacket.

"Bravo, Chaplin!" a few people shout. Roses fly into our box. A little distance away sits an elegant, gray-haired young man with a slender, intelligent face. It is Chaplin. He looks over to us and laughs.

"Lerle, I have to meet Chaplin! I have a terrific film idea for him."

Loos knows that Chaplin is very reserved. He does not want to overwhelm him and so writes a letter to a common friend, the writer Hollriegel, in Vienna. In the meantime, Loos is pleased to see Chaplin at the beach everyday. He often says in reproach to an acquaintance: "Chaplin just turned around again to look at us. You really ought to wear a pair of trousers that has a less baggy bottom. I am sure Chaplin will copy you in his next film and wear your baggy trousers!"

Hollriegel sends no reply. Loos sighs. "Hopefully Chaplin won't leave before I have had a chance to talk to him. My film idea is this: Years ago when I was in America, I went to eat at a buffet, but I did not have more than 10 cents in my pocket. In America they have large bowls filled with compote; for 10 cents, you can eat as much as you want. You pay when you leave. As bad luck would have it, my 10 cents falls into the compote. I try desperately to fish it out with the big spoon, but it is no use. And so I eat and eat under the scathing glare of the owner until the bowl is empty and I have retrieved my money. Based on this true story Chaplin could make a terrific comedy. The guests watching in amazement, the owner wants to take the container away from him, he fights him, his desperation, his fear, the searching with the big spoon... All of that would be an idea for a film for Chaplin."

The letter from Hollriegel finally comes, but too late. Chaplin has already left.

KOKOSCHKA IS NO BOCHE

One day, Loos gets hold of a newspaper in which a French critic has written an unfavorable critique of Kokoschka. He talks about his big exhibition in Paris. Among other things, he calls Kokoschka a 'Boche'. Loos, who considers Kokoschka a great painter of our times, is beside himself. After brief consideration, he writes to the editor the following letter:

"Dear Herr Editor!

I would like to point out to you that your article about Kokoschka is inaccurate. The description 'Boche' alone proves this. Even a child can see that the name Kokoschka is not native to Germany. It is that of a Czechoslovak family, which, like so many, later moved to Austria. One of his relatives is even a Czechoslovak general. I thought you should be made aware of this fundamental error."

Loos sends me with this letter to Henri Matisse with the request that he sign it. I travel to Nice that very same day. Henri Matisse lives in a little house not far from the flower market. A plain-looking woman opens the door and leads me into a bright and furnished bourgeois room. Henri Matisse, a friendly man with a white beard, invites me to sit down. The little room is flooded with sunlight. A canary at the window softly sings its tune. Henri Matisse reads the letter; his face looks infinitely kind. With a little smile he hands it back to me.

"Adolf Loos," he says, "is always the same, ready to fight and to sacrifice himself when someone else's honor is at stake. His country, the whole world, can be proud of this man. As far as the critic is concerned, it is really almost an honor to be torn apart by him. All great artists of any stature and renown have been terribly criticized by him! Tell Master Loos that and send him my best regards..."

"Did Matisse sign it?" asks Loos, without paying any attention to anything else Matisse said. "Did he sign?" When I tell him no, he looks at me angrily. "Well then, Lerle, I'll just have to send the letter by myself."

And so he did too.

UISTITI...

A boy, about sixteen years old, walks along the beach with a cage in his hand. A lot of children are following him, crowding around him to take a look in the cage.

Loos jumps up from his lounge chair and beckons to the boy. He comes over to us, followed by the flock of children and a couple of adults too. There are two very tiny monkeys in the cage chattering in high pitch childlike voices. They adeptly do acrobatics on a pole, pausing now and then to look, startled, with their old man eyes at the audience.

"Oh, Lerle, those are Uistiti monkeys," Loos exclaims. "They are charming little animals. I had a pair of such monkeys once years ago. We would let the little monkeys run free during the daytime, they liked to climb around in the trees and would always come back home again in the evening. One day the female caught cold and, despite the most loving care, she died after a few days. The male monkey would not touch any more food after that! He crouched down beside the empty cage. Then something strange happened. I had never thought that such a thing was possible with animals. He climbed up onto the roof and, stiff, let himself fall onto the street. He broke his neck and was dead... he had committed suicide!"

PRINCESS LICHNOWSKY

Princess Lichnowsky had sent her congratulations to Loos, whom she had never met, on his sixtieth birthday.

Loos wants to meet her in person. "I would like to see the woman," he says to me, "who has written a book that expresses my own innermost thoughts and feelings. I could have written 'The Battle with the Specialist'."

The princess is just as delighted to get to know Loos. A horse-drawn carriage takes us to her beautiful villa. A livery servant with white gloves opens the door. The princess, a tall, blond woman with fine but sharp features, walks quickly toward us.

"I am so glad you have come, dear Loos!" she says cordially. We have tea on the terrace with a view of the sea. Next to the princess sits Lurch, a thin gray dog who suspiciously sniffs at our Beau-Beau. Lurch is the hero of her last novel, 'On the Leash'.

A lively conversation is soon in full swing. The princess and Loos are very similar in the way they look at the world. I also find a resemblance between them in their physical appearance.

After tea, the princess takes us into a fairy tale garden. An American millionaire, now living in Japan, had it designed. Narrow winding paths lead up a low rise that softly descends into the sea. Here a grove of orange and lemon trees has been planted. There are also wonderful trees from foreign lands, Japanese bonsai trees and exotic flowers. Loos shows little interest. What he admires most is a tree with golden yellow trumpet blossoms, which are so-called because each blossom resembles a swinging, yellow, mail coach horn. He devotes his attention however, to Lurch, the novel hero, and a small, charming, brown dachshund.

We stay until evening falls, and affectionately say goodbye. In return for her kindness, Loos sends the princess a large, golden-yellow Provençal jug of honey, the type sold by the local peasants.

HOW LOOS GETS A PROJECT AND A PORTRAIT

A lady and a gentleman walk in. The lady is very pretty, redheaded with dark eyes. "W. X." mutters the gentleman, a tall slender man.

"We read in the newspaper that you were here, Herr Loos," he says, "and since I am Viennese too, I wanted to come and see you. "

"Pleased to meet you! Is your wife Viennese too?"

"My wife is French; she does not understand much German."

"That is too bad," says Loos. "Do you speak English? Unfortunately, I do not speak French," he adds, smiling.

W. X. is a sculptor. He asks Loos to sit for him for a portrait. Loos cordially agrees. We now get together with the young couple fairly often. They are living in a charming little apartment in Nice. In the living room they have put down gray linen with cherry red borders, which covers the floor up to the walls.

Whilst Loos sits for the portrait, we prepare lunch in the tiny kitchen adjacent to the living room. Sometimes we also go for a swim down at the beach.

One day W. X. brings some house plans with him. One of his relatives owns a magnificent villa on the Promenade des Anglais. To rent out such a villa is difficult, to sell it impossible. He would like to make use of this villa somehow.

Loos immediately takes a trip to Nice to see the villa. He likes it very much indeed. He does not want to change anything; he always has respect for the work of a colleague whom he admires. But he does have a wonderful idea: the villa is not situated directly on the street, there is a garden in front of it. Loos would like to extend the lowest terrace out to the edge of the street.

"There is room here for a nice coffee house," he says. He also adapts part of the inner hall for this purpose, the remainder of the villa could be rented out. Since the terrace is somewhat elevated, rooms can be created beneath it, which, although partially subterranean, could be used in the evenings or in the event it rained. The owner has the plans sent to him but hesitates to have them carried out. When asked what he owes Loos, he replies, "10 percent if and when you have it built, and one cup of free coffee every day thereafter!" He is especially looking forward to the coffee.

The portrait of Loos is nearing completion.

"I think I'll have it cast in bronze," says W. X. "It will be more impressive in bronze."

"If the portrait is good, the material does not matter," grumbles Loos. "Why bronze? That is way too expensive!"

"I can certainly let you have it for less money if it is in plaster," says the artist.

"What did you say? Let me have it? Did I ever tell you I would want you to let me have it? And for less money? You are asking me for money?! You should pay me something for sitting for you. Very few people have been granted that honor, my dear sir!"

Only the repeated assurance that it was all a misunderstanding calms Loos down. A picture of the portrait was published later on in the Prager Presse. I do not know what happened to it. After that, I did not hear anything more from W. X. and his charming wife.

LOOS AND BEAU-BEAU

Beau-Beau is ill. The most lovable of all dogs stares at his master with big sad eyes. He drags himself around painfully. Loos gets a cab and we drive to the veterinarian.

"Well," he says after the examination, "he probably ate something bad. Don't let him run around free and only give him rice to eat."

"Poor dog," says Loos sadly.

We drive back. Beau-Beau cowers either on the lap of his master or under his seat. He completely ignores me. The weather is wonderful for bathing. I swim far out. Who do I see running toward me with his tail wagging and his nose full of sand? Beau-Beau the dog!

"Well, Dolf, why did you let him run free?"

Loos makes a guilty face. "I couldn't stand, Lerle, to watch the dog pining! He wanted to run free... Just see how happy he is now!"

"Yes," I argue, "and now he is eating sand!"

"A dog has more instinct than a human. The sand will cure him!"

A few days later, he has another attack. Loos is miserable. We take a taxi again and drive to the veterinarian.

He makes a very concerned face. "It's the falling sickness," he says, "the dog needs to have shots. He has to stay here. I have a dog sanatorium."

"I am happy to pay more than the usual fee," says Loos. "But, please, treat him well!"

We drive home, worried. Loos has no peace. He drives out every day to see Beau-Beau.

Our departure is sudden, as always. It is out of question to take Beau-Beau along. But Loos says:

"I simply do not have it in my heart to leave Beau-Beau in the sanatorium. He isn't at all lively anymore, he hardly even wags his tail when we come. That is not the illness, oh no. Beau-Beau is getting melancholic because of his depressing surroundings."

"Couldn't we give him to W. X.?" I ask timidly.

"To W. X.?" Loos is enthusiastic about the idea.

Frau X. loves Beau-Beau like a child. She also has another dog. She will take care of him and love him.

Shortly after our arrival in Paris comes a letter from W. X. Beau-Beau is very sick, he will never be completely well again. Never again! Loos holds his breath for a moment, then writes a telegram: "Have Beau-Beau put to sleep immediately!" – "I love him too much, I want to spare him the suffering! Never be healthy again! I could not bear that thought."

OUR TRIP TO PARIS

Loos is studying the timetables. Never is a trip undertaken without having carefully gone over all possible trains. Loos is the ideal man for organizing a trip. This time, we are travelling back to Paris. Loos finds trains from small local railways that run through the mountains to Lyon.

"I want to get to know the country and the people," he responds to my objection that these trains are probably very uncomfortable.

The trip is uniquely beautiful. Mulberry trees, deciduous forests, unusual flowers grow in the stony ground. The train takes us up, higher and higher. The mountain and the valley remind me of the Semmering area, shepherds with herds of sheep move along the mountain roads.

The train stops at every small station. Peasants and country folk carrying baskets and bags get off and on, chatting animatedly. I can hardly understand them. The language is similar to Italian. The people are dark-eyed and handsome. We are the only foreigners in these trains. A friendly farmer helps me to load and unload our burdensome luggage.

We change trains often. We travel slowly past old farmhouses with large curved gates.

"Here, I want to learn," says Loos. "Only once I know

enough about the country, the people, and the customs, which are influenced by the terrain, would I attempt to build here."

A new valley opens in front of us. The stone houses nestled up against the rocky cliffs seem to be a part of the cliffs themselves.

"And one has to find out what type of building material is cheapest and the easiest to obtain here in order to save money, labor and time."

We spend one night in a small village, the name of which I have forgotten. There are two seats left in the old-fashioned yellow stagecoach that seems to have come straight out of a children's fairy tale book. The inn, sheltered by blooming chestnut trees, is simple and clean.

Loos immediately starts a lengthy conversation with the innkeepers. He soon finds out that one can stay here in the summer for 15 francs a day; also that people from Paris actually do come to stay here. Yes, an omnibus drives three times a week through the mountains to southern France and back to Paris. Loos asks about the price of groceries, some of which have to be brought in from far away because the soil is so rocky here. He asks and asks and the wife of the innkeeper is delighted that this stranger should take such an interest in her life. She willingly provides the information until Loos knows everything, even their private life and habits.

Then, he the never-tiring, orders us each a glass of wine. Sitting beneath the chestnut trees, we watch the children playing on the village square. After taking a short rest, Loos tours the village, studies the old buildings and houses and lingers a while in the church that stands partially in ruin.

Lyon. We spend two hours there, from ten to twelve o'clock at night. The air of this industrial city is oppressive after all the sunlit fresh air. We stroll through the city, which is not very alive. There are many taverns here. We eat dinner and drink a wonderful glass of beer in a simple lounge.

A blond man who works in a silk factory is happy to give us some information about the city and the people. Loos has him give us a detailed description of silk and its manufacturing. I have the impression that this industrial city does not offer much in the way of intellectual life and is probably quite provincial.

At one o'clock we are already in our sleeping car compartment. The train is almost empty. Loos smiles contentedly.

"See, Lerle, how silly people are! This train, the only one which has second class sleeping cars, is hardly occupied." Loos is really the born travel marshal.

Five o'clock in the morning. The conductor knocks. In a quarter of an hour we will be in Paris. "Ach," murmurs Loos, "that is the end station, the worst that can happen to us is that we will be put off onto a sidetrack." He goes back to sleep. Five minutes before the train is to arrive he leaps out of bed. He is completely changed.

"Lerle," he calls out, "we are arriving in Paris!" Standing in front of the mirror he meticulously knots his tie. And because it does not turn out nice enough, he ties it again. Paris... Paris.

A taxi takes us through the awakening city to Montparnasse. Loos has the driver stop in front of the Café du Dôme. Our seven suitcases, small trunks and dressing cases are unloaded in front of the Café. Loos sits down at one of the iron tables, smiling contentedly. The old waiter, who knows him, comes happily over to him.

"One oatmeal as usual," Loos orders. Under the table, two drunks are snoring.

LOOS WANTS TO WORK

Loos has come to Paris to work on a project. In the meantime, the client has reconsidered having the remodelling done. Loos is very upset, does not feel well and stays in bed. The suitcases are lying around his bed, we got them from Kniže, where they were kept in storage. They are full of clothes, but moths have nested and destroyed almost everything. Now they are lying around open here. They give off a musty smell.

"Don't throw them away!" the sick man cries. "Those are still my best clothes in there, don't throw them away."

To put him in a better mood, I bring him some chicken and mayonnaise, which he enjoys eating. Then I hurry to the post office. I come back after an hour. Loos is still lying in bed. In his one hand he has the piece of chicken, in the other the paper with mayonnaise; the whole bed is smeared with mayonnaise.

"Read it," he shouts, "read this letter!" A student writes:

"Herr X. from P. wants me to take charge of a project by myself. Since I am working for you I didn't accept. What should I do?"

I find this letter is very nice and correct.

Loos, on the other hand keeps repeating: "He is stealing my work! He is stealing my work!"

"He is asking you first," I say, agitated, "we can prevent it!"

"Don't prevent it, don't prevent it," cries the sick man. "If the client would prefer to go to the apprentice than to the master it's his own fault, his own fault! Betrayal! Betrayal," Loos groans, "and you too, Lerle, you too!"

He pulls a newspaper page from the bed, takes my hand in an iron grip and points to an article. "It says here that the famous actress Lilian Harvey has finally decided to have her villa built in Nice. Didn't I tell you a hundred times to go and see her? A hundred times, a thousand times! But you are my biggest enemy. You didn't go. Betrayal! Betrayal! You don't want me to work, to build...!"

Suddenly he sits up in bed. His eyes are staring at me, wide-opened and terrible. "Go away!" he screams, "go away, leave me alone! – You will cause me more grief than Josef Hoffmann, my worst enemy! Go away, leave me alone!"

*

I leave. A young painter who we had complained about the day before is standing in front of the building. He gets on my heels and accompanies me. I am so unhappy and so shattered that I hardly even notice him.

Suddenly, a voice next to me says: "Did you know that Loos was much happier and healthier when he lived in

Paris without a wife? A wife hinders a person like Loos –, she destroys him. A woman is an enemy for Loos!"

Every word that the stranger says is like the stab of a dagger to me. Were those not my very own thoughts? "And do you think," I say, shaking, more to myself than to him, "That Loos would be happier if I left him?"

The painter nods. "Absolutely! A genius has to be alone!"

At another time I would have laughed at these words, but now I tremble. The thought of leaving Loos surfaces. But before I carry out this crazy idea, I want to see if the painter is right. I pretend to leave Loos.

Two days later, I see Loos on the arm of his best friend, Oskar Kokoschka, walking through the streets of Paris. His step is lively, he laughs, he is happy...

Many years later, Kokoschka told me: "Back then, Loos came to me in Paris. Tears were pouring from his eyes. He sank, sobbing, into my arms. 'My wife, my wife has left me!'

"'Oh go on,' I said to him, 'that's no great loss, there are lots of women in the world!' And I took his arm and shook him. Loos sighed with tears. Then he pulled himself together, lifted his head up high and walked for hours with me through the streets of Paris."

— — — — — — — — —

I am sitting again in a rattling train, but my thoughts are far away – with Loos. No, I do not want to hurt him, I would rather go away... far away.

Weeks go by. I am living in a daydream. Heavy housework keeps me from thinking. A tremendous apathy has settled over me. I must go back and yet I cannot. My hands have no strength, my thoughts are confused. I cannot undertake anything. But I only need to close my eyes and I am with him – with Loos. Whenever I make the effort to try to shake myself out of it, I hear a cold, merciless voice:

"A woman who has left me may never come back again!"

People take me to my homeland. It makes no difference for me where I live. I only have to close my eyes and I am in my real homeland – with Loos!

*

Loos has some business to take care of in P. where I live.

A sympathetic girlfriend asks me: "Don't you want to go to him? Don't you want to see him?"

See? Really? Not with my eyes closed?

My feet can barely carry me up the hotel steps. I am completely numb. Softly, like a thief, I open the door. He is asleep. I go over to him on tiptoes. I kneel down, trembling with happiness.

"Lerle," he whispers, his eyes still closed. "Lerle..." Then he opens his eyes, closes them, opens them, reaches out to touch me. "Lerle," he calls tenderly. Tears are pouring from his eyes. "Lerle, why did you leave me?"

I bury my face in his hands. "Oh, you," I whisper, crying, "let me be with you forever, then everything will be fine! Don't ask! It was insane... completely insane!"

A voice resounds around me. A voice that I have heard a thousand times in my dreams, I am now really hearing:

"A woman who leaves me may not come back!"

I look at him. Tears are still on his cheeks, but his eyes look clear and unmerciful.

What has happened?

Why is it suddenly so dark in me?

All of the lights in my soul have gone out!

— — — — — — — — — — — —

And that was how life with Adolf Loos ended.

SAYING GOOD-BYE

Loos has been placed in the Rosenhügel Sanatorium in Vienna. He suffered a stroke. My only thought is to see him. Finally I am able to get to Vienna. I arrive at the sanatorium, I ask the porter about Loos; he tells me the ward and room number. Next to him stands a beautiful blond woman. "You want to see Loos," she says, "I ought to tell you, he does not recognize anyone anymore. I am his nurse and have my day off today. When I came back from holiday the day before yesterday, he did not recognize me."

"Please, nurse," I say, "take me to Loos." Walking together a short way, I talk to the nurse. "It is strange," she says, "but because Loos reads newspapers everyday despite his illness, I have got into the habit of doing it too, all in all I have learned quite a lot from Loos. The uniform that I'm wearing, for example, I had it made according to his instructions." We stop in front of a pavilion in the garden. "There," she says, pointing to a window. There indeed, standing at the window, is Loos, held up left and right under his arms by doctors. He looks blankly off into space. Suddenly his eyes fall on me, on the nurse, and then back on me. A smile slides quickly over his rigid face. Then he tears an arm loose, points to me and says clearly and plainly: "Lerle." I run into the building, I try to look happy and radiant, he is not supposed to notice that his condition is affecting me. He motions as if making an introduction to the doctors and says, "my wife" then whispers to me a little joking comment. At that moment he is quite his old self again. Then – as it is apparent that speaking is quite a strain for him – he takes a pencil and writes: "Heidelberg, Mannheim, Stuttgart, Zurich. Milan – our trip." Then he points to me, to himself, to the door. He wants to go away, go far away with me, to the south. I help him into a wheelchair and push him out into the garden. He takes my hand and is pleased, he laughs, he is happy. The time passes all too quickly. I have to leave, I let him know that I will come back again soon. Loos looks at me, there is an infinite sadness on his face, he takes both my hands and presses them to his chest. His lips whisper something unintelligible. "Oh, yes, yes, I will certainly come again tomorrow." I nod. But he only slowly shakes his head, as if he knew better. I leave. Down by the gate I stop and look back up to him. He is sitting up straight in the wheelchair, motionless. He does not speak, he does not wave, he looks towards me...

Appendices

ADOLF LOOS' CIRCLE, SOME CONTEXT

KARL KRAUS (April 28, 1874 – June 12, 1936) was a Viennese writer, satirist, publisher of the controversial *Die Fackel* (*The Torch*), and one of Loos' closest friends. He is best known for his defense of language and indicting hypocrisy in all manner of Viennese and Imperial society, but later was criticized for his uncritical use of anti-Semitic clichés, and for supporting the idea that Austrians should abolish all traces of Hebrew in their German and bring the language closer to a "pure" German. Kraus later began reassessing those positions as Nazis rose to power, and he soon began a scathing critique against German politics. Subsequently his works were banned during the Third Reich. Karl Kraus converted from Judaism to Catholicism in 1911 with Adolf Loos as his sole witness. Kraus was related to Claire Beck Loos by a marriage between his brother Alfred Kraus and Claire's father Otto Beck's cousin Rosa Hirsch.

OSKAR KOKOSCHKA (March 1, 1886 – February 22, 1980) was an Austrian painter and close friend of Adolf Loos. It is said that Loos advised all of his clients to buy a Kokoschka painting for their homes, including the Becks, who had a large painting hanging in their dining room. Otto Beck's cousin Wilhelm and his wife Martha Hirsch both commissioned portraits by Kokoschka. Martha, one of his more well-known sitters, was known to dislike Kokoschka's painting of her, entitled *Dreaming Woman* (1909);

later, Nazis used this painting to vilify Kokoschka, citing it as an example of his "degenerate art."

PRINCESS LICHNOWSKY, or Mechthilde Lichnowsky, (March 8, 1879 – June 4, 1958) was the granddaughter of Empress Maria Theresa of Austria and wife of Karl Max, Prince Lichnowsky, the German diplomat to England from 1912–1914. Mechthilde Lichnowsky wrote eighteen books, in addition to poetry and works for theatre. Among her literary cohorts was Karl Kraus. During the Second World War she was considered a traitor by the Nazis and suffered her books being burnt; however, she was later considered a Nazi accomplice by the communist Czech government and thus was expelled and all of her family's property seized. One of the books she wrote, mentioned by Claire that Loos himself felt an affinity with, *The Battle with the Specialist*, took on all manner of self-conferred "experts" from train conductors to doctors to people with pompous and obnoxious attitudes.

ERICH MARIA REMARQUE (June 22, 1898 – September 25, 1970) was a German writer who authored nearly twenty books. He was conscripted into the German army during World War One and wrote about these experiences in the novel *All Quiet on the Western Front* in 1927 (published in 1929). Later, Remarque's books were banned by the Nazis and many of his family suffered under their regime. He wrote the following letter to Loos while at the Hotel du Cap D'Antibes in 1931, which Claire kept, and which has been reprinted here with the permission of the Erich Maria Remarque-Friedenszentrum in Osnabrück, Germany. It has been translated by the Friedenszentrum's Thomas Schneider.

> Dear and admired Herr Loos:
> I was shattered by your great work, by the lucidity and beauty of your ideas and by the variety and intensity of your creative power — but more shattered by the fact that stupidity, malice and the average were successful for decades in concealing this work — With the wish to get to know a lot more about you, I am Yours sincerely,
> Erich Maria Remarque

JOSEPH ROTH (September 2, 1894 – May 27, 1939) was a Jewish Austrian journalist and author born in what is now known as the Ukraine. He detailed the paths of the Jewish diaspora in Europe after World War One and the Russian Revolution. The subject of his novel *Radetzky March* (1932) is the decline and fall of the Hapsburg Empire.

EMIL LUDWIG (January 25, 1881 – September 17, 1948) was a writer and journalist who interviewed many political figures including Stalin and Ataturk. He wrote for the *Wiener Freie Presse* and the *Berliner Tageblatt* and is known for his insightful biographies.

BOHUMIL MARKALOUS (Jaromír John) (April 16, 1882 – April 24, 1952) was a Czechoslovak journalist and author who lived in Prague. He published an article in 1924/1925 in *Wohnungkultur* [*Apartment Culture*] entitled: "Adolf Loos: Man of Our Time." He helped organize the celebration of Loos' sixtieth birthday at the Společenský club about which Claire writes.

JAN SLIVINSKI (Hans Effenberger) was a writer and book-seller whom Loos visited in Paris. Slivinski's circle of intellectuals included artists and Polish refugees.

MARCEL RAY was a German writer, part of the Berlin circle of Dadaists. While not much biographical information can be easily found about Ray, he was well known for his 1927 book *George Grosz: Peintres et Sculptures*, a monograph.

JOSEF SVATOPLUK MACHAR (Februrary 29, 1864 – March 17, 1942) was a Czechoslovak essayist and a leader of the realist movement in poetry. He espoused anti-Austrian views and the emancipation of women. His influence is felt widely in Czechoslovak poetry.

Machar wrote a brief letter to Claire on August 19, 1932, the unstated subject of which likely had to do with the fundraising efforts for Loos' tomb.

> Madame,
>
> I have tried this and that but to no avail. I hope that Dr. Markalous will have more luck. The times are horrible, the so-called crisis is

everywhere. I don't know if Herr Doctor Masaryk wanted to do something — our 40-year friendship has gone to pieces.

A dismal letter, no? But ...

Yours faithfully,

S. Machar

ARNOLD HÖLLRIEGEL (Richard Arnold Bermann) was an Austrian writer who made his name in Berlin between the two World Wars writing non-fiction and novels, and was on the staff at *Die Stunde* [*The Hour*] where he wrote arts and travel articles. He went to America in the twenties and befriended Charlie Chaplin. He later became a leader for the German Academy of Arts and Sciences in Exile after Hitler came to power.

HEINRICH KULKA (March 29, 1900 – May 9, 1971) Loos' student and then later, associate, carried out many of his projects including his Werkbundsiedlung houses in Vienna, which Claire mentions. He published the first Loos monograph *Adolf Loos: Das Werk des Architekten* in 1931.

ZLATKO NEUMANN (March 4, 1900 – January 9, 1969) One of Loos' most trusted collaborators, a Croatian architect, who also served as proxy on Loos projects.

GIUSEPPE DE FINETTI (March 5, 1892 – January 19, 1952) The sole Italian student of Adolf Loos, credited with shaping contemporary Milan.

KURT UNGER was a student and, later, assistant to Loos. Among the work he did for Loos were plans for Dr. Josef Fleischner's villa in Haifa. He also managed the production of Loos' design work in glass and tableware, and became a financial supporter in Loos' last years.

KEY TO NAMES˙

* P. (pages 41, 177, 180) – Pilsen

"A second Kobenzl" (page 46) – Hotel Kobenzl in Salzburg

* "One of my girlfriends, ... who is now working for Loos" (page 54) – Ilse Günther (von Hennig), who worked with Loos on commissions for the Tzara, Moller, Khuner, and Müller houses.

* General K. (pages 56, 121–123) – General Klecanda

* Client B. (pages 64, 106) – Hans Brummel, Pilsen

* Frau X. (page 66) – Genia Schwarzwald

* Client X. (page 79) – Dr. Gustav Scheu

* Pension Z. (page 87) – Pension Zenz is located on the Alserstrasse in Vienna.

The artist Kolo Moser (page 89) is Koloman Moser, who founded the Wiener Werkstätte in 1903 with Loos' archrival Josef Hoffmann.

* The big exhibition abroad (page 101) mentioned in the

---

* Items denoted with * have been reprinted from Loos, Claire Beck. *Adolf Loos Privat.* Adolf Opel, ed. (Vienna: Böhlau 1985).

chapter "I Am a Cosmopolitan" took place at the end of 1930 in Milan.

* Concerning Loos' citizenship (page 101) – he chose Austrian citizenship after the collapse of the monarchy and did not accept Czechoslovak citizenship until later in life and only then in addition to his Austrian citizenship.

Masaryk (page 103) – Tomáš Garrigue Masaryk was the founder and first President of Czechoslovakia, who granted Loos a regular government honorarium upon his sixtieth birthday.

Machar (page 103) – Czechoslovak national poet Josef Svatopluk Machar

Starhemberg (page 108) – Ernst Rüdiger Camillo Starhemberg was a conservative Austrian nationalist politician, who had contact with the early Nazi movement of the 1920s but after Hitler's failed coup d'etat (the Beer Hall Putsch), rejected the movement. As vice chancellor during Vienna's civil war in 1934, Starhemberg fought to keep Austria free from a Nazi takeover.

* Doctor X. (pages 109–114) – Dr. Oskar Simon was the owner of the Esplanade Sanatorium in Karlsbad that Loos remodelled in 1930–1931.

Hotel Babylon in Nice (page 132) – Loos designed the hotel in 1923, but it was never built. He took the name from a popular novel by Arnold Bennett, The Grand Babylon Hotel. It was to have one thousand beds in seven hundred hotel rooms, a gigantic building. Loos wrote,

> Each hotel must be designed to meet the needs of its setting. I
> decided on the Riviera, which I know well. But each hotel ought

also to be designed for a particular class of society. Structural shortcomings, however, make this impossible. Dark rooms facing the yard must be let off cheaply even in luxury hotels. A hotel, set back on terracing, however, has no such rooms: it has only front rooms. In addition, by means of girder construction (i.e., by the use of structural steel) the east, west and sunny sides can be elongated. The main thing is that each room has its own terrace. [...]

If we compare the project with two linked pyramids, we may speak of two enormous sepulchral vaults. One of these is to be designed as an ice palace, the other as a large ballroom. Between the two there is a large top-lit room which – instead of a glass roof, which would not be a pretty sight from the inner terraces – is to be given a water tank with a Luxfer [prism] floor."[*]

Bernhard Shaw (page 152) is the Irish playwright and author George Bernhard Shaw.

* Furniture store S. (page 159) – Schurmann Brothers Furniture Store in Berlin

* The exposition mentioned (page 159) is the 1931 International Interior Decoration Exposition in Cologne.

* Herr W. X. (page 168) – sculptor Francis Wills

* A picture of the portrait bust of Adolf Loos by Francis Wills (pages 168–170) was printed in the pictorial supplement of the Prager Presse on July 12, 1931. June 1931 is cited in the picture's caption as the date of completion.

---

* Quoted in Münz, Ludwig and Gustav Künstler. *Adolf Loos, Pioneer of Modern Architecture* (London: Thames & Hudson, 1966) 134–136.

The German spellings Claire used for Czechoslovak places have been retained in this edition. Czech names are included below:

Laurenziberg – Petřín

Hradshin – Hradčany

Brunn – Brno

Pilsen – Plzeň

Thomas Baťa – Tomáš Baťa

ERRATA

The 2011 hardcover edition of this book (*Adolf Loos — A Private Portrait,* DoppelHouse Press, 2011) contains errors in an appendix section titled "Notes on Claire and Loos' Divorce and Beck-Schanzer Family History," regarding payments from Claire's brother-in-law Stefan Schanzer to Adolf Loos. The facts were revealed in 2012 and are elaborated in *Escape Home: Rebuilding a Life After the Anschluss* by Claire's nephew, Charles Paterson (DoppelHouse Press, 2013). In the end, Schanzer turns out to have been a Loos client rather than a tenant or benefactor. The supporting documentation was discovered in the Albertina Loos archive by architecture scholars Otto Kapfinger and Andreas Nierhaus. On the reverse of Loos' plans for what has been known generically as the "Einfamilienhaus" are pencil marks in Loos' handwriting indicating "Haus Schanzer."

LOVE LETTERS FROM ADOLF LOOS TO CLAIRE BECK BEFORE THEIR MARRIAGE, 1929*

Friday, February 15, 7:30 p.m., Café Waldeck [the most distinguished hotel in Pilsen] to Claire in Vienna:

Dear Claire, your parents have just left. When I will have finished this letter, I will meet them again for dinner. Later on I will go to the bar with Brummels and, probably, Hirsch [two Loos clients from Pilsen, the latter, related to Claire]. I hope that you have done everything to my satisfaction. It will not function successfully because you don't follow my directions, i.e. the dog picture. Again: Call Dr. Ermers concerning the tile. After that, get in touch with Elsie [Loos' second wife]. Ask for the book. Borrow the book and demand that Lányi [an art and book dealer in Vienna] buy it. Then carry both and the letters to K.K. [presumably Karl Kraus]. Maybe you can tell Ms. Helene Kann to do that. You'll find her address in the telephone book.

Dear Claire, don't even think about leaving me now. Wait a little bit. The time I take from you is not lost for you. It is the first time in my life that I have found a woman who doesn't demand that I live for her, but is willing to live for me. I have lived such a dull life up until now! Was it the meaning of my life that someone prances as a soubrette at the "Theater an der Wien"? The world would have derived much more benefit from me if I had found a protectress, a nurse like you. Nevertheless,

* Rukschcio, Burkhardt and Roland Schachel. *Adolf Loos — Leben und Werk* (Vienna: Residenz Verlag, 1982) 343, 348–349.

it was my fault. P.A. [Peter Altenberg] has said very often that I spoil all the women rather than making them happy. I should have said: Getting married, yes, but stop the prancing about.

Farewell, my secretary and my nanny.

Gratefully yours, Dolf

'Bye 'bye, but who knows if the train will arrive, here everything comes apart at the seams when it is cold. Next Monday the factories will close.

Undated:

My dear Lärle, I am an old donkey and I have cried like a little child. If you cannot get the passport for me, I have no idea what to do. Will they take care of my birth certificate as well as my registration certificate? If not, steal those documents and get a new passport. Let me know where we can meet in Prague. From Prague I will go to Pilsen. What does your father want to do in Vienna? Don't bother me with your jealousy! I miss you very much, and I am almost deaf. In the future, I will come to Prague quite often, you are not out of this world. But I will not hear your sweet saxophone voice anymore, day by day I am getting more deaf. Your father is right – I am a deaf cripple. I will be very grateful for every day you want to stay with me. Another thing: K.K. [Karl Kraus] won't take the paintings/pictures ["Bilder"]. But I am looking forward to seeing you.

Yours, Dolf

April 23rd, from a coffeehouse in Pilsen:

Lerle, sweety, I thank you that you have thought of me in three letters. I thought, you, as a good daughter of your father, had forgotten me. Today I met your father, he is well, but he has sleepless nights because of you. I told him it would be very convenient if you became my secretary. Everything fine. But he said you would be too good for that. You have to marry a young man, then everything will be fine in the marriage. He will find this young man, I guess. I told him, he should not think so much. 'A man who doesn't know to go where, will come farthest', Cromwell the revolutionary says. I have promised him [your father] by handshake, that I will never hinder you from getting married if he finds somebody. The both of us are best friends. He is completely right about me. I will send a wire when I come.

I have to finish now, Mrs. Vogel [a Loos client] will pick me up at any moment. I am fine, my little hero!

Kisses, Dolf

June 25th, from Café Imperial in Vienna:

My dear Lerle, what a beautiful letter I have received from you! I would like to publish it to the whole world, all the people should participate in my happiness. Nobody will believe what a nice wife I will get. The letter is a great poem in prose. If only I could write so beautiful [sic.]! The drops of jealousy are a compliment, but after marriage I don't need compliments anymore...

But dear Lerle is missed here. Farewell my Lerle, I am honest, don't be jealous, everything is for you...

Thousands of kisses everywhere, your husband Dolf.

Thursday, July 4th:

My beloved Lerle, I thank you for the nice letter, I feel sorry for you for the sorrows you are having on my behalf.

But I don't have the problems Beer has, definitely not. I need only jobs, not money. This [money] comes on its own. I don't want to get in contact with somebody like Beer. I told you that I want to draw the line. The line is marked by round windows. I think that all architects who make round windows in a time of traverses and ferroconcrete are tricksters. Why should I be in contact with inferior humans?

I don't feel well. I am tired, and if this feeling remains, I cannot live much longer. I am really old. Are the tablets the reason for this? I have taken 13 ½ pills, not more. Tomorrow I will take nine [pills], for three days. I don't have pain, I am only tired!

Poor Klärle! But I console myself, either I will recover or you will become a widow soon.

This cannot last.

I don't talk to anybody and I am glad about it. I think I am nearly deaf.

I send you The Stage [a periodical]. The [serial] novel they have included is interesting. You could have written the novel. I will send you the next part. I also send you the foreigner's list. The wife of the chimney sweep belongs to the upper society.

Besides there are a lot of Jews in kaftans and plain clothes. I have the feeling, when they are at home they take off the kaftan. But I like them more than the people from Vienna.

Dear Lerle, I feel very sorry for you. Why did you fall in love with me? Who knows, if it is bad for you. People should have left us alone, but they tried to separate us. Now we get married [sic.]. I hope everything will get different [sic.].

Your husband kisses you intensively.

Undated:

Dear Lerle, today, Saturday, I received two letters, yesterday none: But what do you think: If we get married, we will do it as soon as we can. I will leave in the evening, we will get married in the late morning, in the early afternoon we will leave again. This way I lose only one day gurgling and drinking. I should take a bath only every second day anyway. I took a bath today. Most important thing is that all papers [marriage certifications] are here. On the last day [there's] always one piece is missing. I have finished an article for the Frankfurter [Zeitung, the newspaper] about David Roentgen, a carpenter from 18th century.

What is it about my mouth? Do you think, I will become mute? Maybe, the cure won't change anything.

Did you receive my letter I have written before I left?

I can't wait, tell Knöpfelmacher he should hurry!

Heartfelt kissing... Yours, Dolf

Thanks for the 209 shillings.

Adolf Loos and Claire Beck, 1928. Published in Loos, Claire Beck. *Adolf Loos Privat*. ed. Adolf Opel (Vienna: Böhlau, 1985). Photographer unattributed.

Adolf Loos in his living room inglenook at his apartment, Giselastrasse 3
(now Bösendorferßtrasse), Vienna I, circa 1929.

CLAIRE BECK

FRAU ADOLF LOOS

ABOVE LEFT
Claire Beck, experimental self-portrait, circa mid-late 1920s.
STUDY AND DOKUMENTATION
CENTRUM, VILLA MÜLLER, PRAGUE

ABOVE RIGHT
Calling cards for Claire Beck Loos, before and after her marriage to Adolf Loos, circa mid-late 1920s.
PATERSON FAMILY ARCHIVE

RIGHT
Claire Beck, studio portrait, circa mid-1920s.
PATERSON FAMILY ARCHIVE

The Beck family in their hackney carriage, circa 1909. LEFT TO RIGHT Unidentified driver and dog, Eva Beck, Olga Feigl Beck, and Claire Beck, who is seated on the lap of her father, Otto Beck. Photographer unattributed. PATERSON FAMILY ARCHIVE

Postcard to Otto Beck's brother Robert Beck. LEFT TO RIGHT Olga Feigl Beck with her children, Max, Claire, and Eva Beck in Carinthia, Austria, 1913. PATERSON FAMILY ARCHIVE

ABOVE New Year's Eve dinner at the Becks' first Loos-designed apartment, Klattauerstrasse 12, Pilsen, 1927. LEFT TO RIGHT Eva Beck Schanzer, Stefan Schanzer, Otto Beck, Olga Feigl Beck, and Max Beck. PHOTO CLAIRE BECK

BELOW New Year's Eve party at the second Loos-designed Beck apartment, Benešplatz 2, Pilsen, December 31, 1929. Otto Beck (center), Max Beck (right); Olga Beck (on chair), Adolf Loos (sitting, second from right), and Claire's best friend, Ilse Günther (sitting, right). PHOTO CLAIRE BECK LOOS

BOTH IMAGES PATERSON FAMILY ARCHIVE

204

Olga Beck and unidentified friend admiring Olga's birthday gifts of shoes and gloves. Photograph taken in the living room of the Loos-designed apartment at Benešplatz 2, Pilsen, June 4, 1934. Of note is that all chairs are different, conforming to Adolf Loos' philosophy of personal comfort in interior design.

LEFT TO RIGHT Otto Beck, Max Beck, family friend, and Olga Beck.

PHOTO CLAIRE BECK LOOS; PATERSON FAMILY ARCHIVE

ABOVE Claire and Loos' marriage in Vienna on July 18, 1929. This photo was relatively unknown for nearly fifty years until Max Beck gave it to editor Adolf Opel for the republication of *Adolf Loos Privat* in 1985. Photographer unattributed.

LEFT TO RIGHT Mitzi Schnabl, Loos' housekeeper; Bořijov Kriegerbeck, Loos' carpenter and contractor in Czechoslovakia; Claire; Loos; Heinrich Kulka, an architect, collaborator, and former student of Loos; and Claire's mother Olga Beck. Otto Beck refused to attend, though Loos does write to Claire that at least he will be invited for lunch. Courtesy Janet Beck Wilson

PATERSON FAMILY ARCHIVE

OPPOSITE Claire Beck, studio photograph taken in Prague, date unknown, presumably sent to Adolf Loos during their courtship.
Courtesy Burkhardt Rukschcio

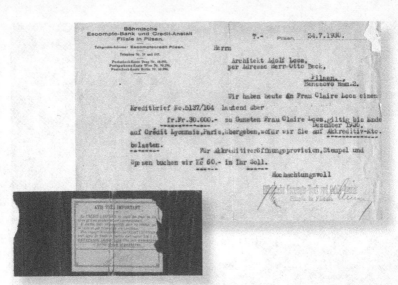

ABOVE

Notice of extension of credit in the amount of 30,000 francs on July 24, 1930, from Otto Beck's bank in Pilsen to Adolf Loos, care of Claire Beck Loos at Crédit Lyonnaise in Paris.

The amount would later be at issue in Claire and Loos' divorce, with Otto Beck demanding Loos return the money spent, which Loos offered instead to parry into an architectural commission. Otto then suggested Loos turn over his apartment in Vienna to Claire. The issue remained unresolved. After Loos' death, executor Elsie Altmann-Loos, Loos' second wife, refused to let Claire live there.

BELOW

Postcard from one of Loos' Viennese contractors, Kremser, thought to be a wallpaperer (Rukschcio and Schachel, 1982), and addressed to Loos c/o Kniže men's outfitters, forwarded to Loos and Claire at the Hotel Regina.

PATERSON FAMILY ARCHIVE

Le Ier Octobre I930

Chère Madame,

J'ai eu hier soir une longue conversation avec un de mes amis qui est l'administrateur d'un banque très importante et le projet d'élever une maison de M. LOOS à PARIS l'intéresse beaucoup. Mais pour celà j'ai besoin de toute urgence des choses suivantes:

les plans détaillés du groupe de maisons envisagé avec les <u>dimensions</u> de ce groupe, le nombre de maisons, la hauteur de ces maisons; etc...

l'emplacement que préférerait M. LOOS pour l'édification de ces maisons.

Ainsi que je vous l'ai dit dans ma dernière lettre j'ai écrit à la Maison de Vienne qui m'avait envoyé la photographie du groupe pour lui demander les plans détaillés. J'espère les avoir bientôt.

Je serais très content d'avoir de vos nouvelles bientôt et je vous prie de croire, chère Madame, à l'expression de ma respectueuse amitié. Veuillez, je vous en prie, présenter mes respectueuses salutations à M. LOOS .

Letter from a potential Loos client, Jean LeBeuf, to Claire Beck Loos about a possible housing project in Paris, for which LeBeuf would like details as soon as possible and extends his wishes and friendship respectfully to Adolf Loos, October 1, 1930.

Adolf Loos' sixtieth birthday, Villa Müller, Prague, December 10, 1930.

LEFT TO RIGHT, standing: architect Josef Gočár, Baron Karl Nádherný von Borutin;

LEFT TO RIGHT, seated: Dr. Ing. František Müller, Claire Beck Loos, Milada Müller, Adolf Loos, Karl Kraus, Baroness Sidonie Nádherný von Borutin, Baroness Valentine Mladota-Codelli-Lumbe, Countess Maria Dobrzensky von Dobrzenicz;

RIGHT SIDE, standing: Count Dobrzensky von Dobrzenicz (?), Baron Mladota von Solopisk (?). Published in Rukschcio and Schachel. *Adolf Loos — Leben und Werk.*

Adolf Loos and Claire Beck Loos at Loos' sixtieth birthday celebration at the
Společenský club, Prague, December 10, 1930.
Photographer unattributed.
Courtesy Burkhardt Rukschcio

ABOVE AND BOTTOM RIGHT Portrait study of Adolf Loos (with his dog Kiki) in his Vienna apartment, circa 1929. PHOTOS CLAIRE BECK LOOS; THE ALBERTINA MUSEUM, VIENNA

BOTTOM LEFT Claire Beck Loos (perhaps holding their dog Beau-Beau) with female onlooker over her shoulder, circa 1930; Photograph possibly by Adolf Loos during their trip in the south of France. Courtesy Burkhardt Rukschcio

Claire Beck Loos and Adolf Loos, Stuttgart, Germany, 1931. Published in
Adolf Loos Privat, 1985.
Photo by Gustav Schleicher, a former student of Loos.

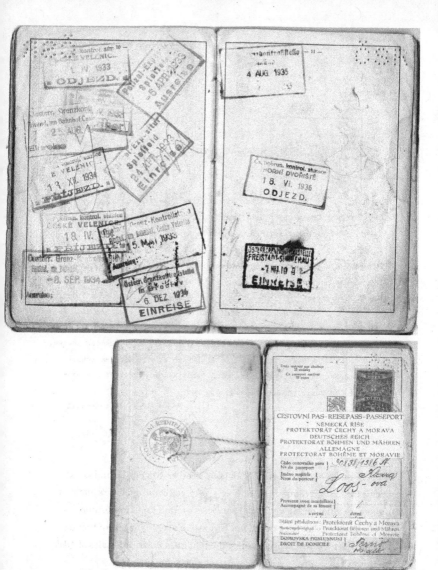

Passport of Claire Beck Loos during the span of time before and after Nazi invasion of Czechoslovakia. A faint stamp on the top left page indicates she entered Austria on August 25, 1933, likely to attend the funeral for Loos, who died on August 23. Another page shows her returning to Czechoslovakia on the same day.

Courtesy Janet Beck Wilson

Pilsen, 3.Dezember 1936

Herrn

Dr. Ludwig M ü n z ,

W i e n .

Sehr geehrter Herr Doktor! (*Münz*)

Meine Schwester Frau Claire Loos teilt mir mit,
dass sie,auf Grund einer Unterredung mit Ihnen,bereit ist,Ihnen
ihre Forderungen gegen die Neue Galerie Wien I. Grünangergasse 1,
aus dem Titel Autorenhonorar von 15 % von brochierten,verkauften
Exemplaren , Loos privat, zu übertragen
Eingehende Beträge sind als Beitrag zum Ankauf des Grabsteines für
Adolf Loos gedacht.

Meine Schwester wird jedoch nicht dafür haften,dass die
diese Forderungen tatsächlich eingehen und haftet auch nicht für
Ihnen etwa durch die Eintreibung dieser Forderung entstehenden Kosten.

Bitte wollen Sie mir mitteilen,ob Sie mit dem Inhalt
dieses Schreibens einverstanden sind,damit meine Schwester ein ent-
sprechendes Schreiben an Sie absenden kann.

Hochachtungsvoll

Correspondence between Claire Beck Loos' brother, Max Beck, and Loos
collector Dr. Ludwig Münz on December 3, 1936, confirming Claire's intention
to donate royalties on sales of *Adolf Loos Privat* to fund Loos' tombstone.
Another letter to Max Beck from Otto Nirenstein's Neue Galerie in Vienna
regarding the 1020 initial print run by the Johannes Presse and sales of *Adolf
Loos Privat* shows a little over 300 copies sold by October 23, 1936.
Courtesy Janet Beck Wilson

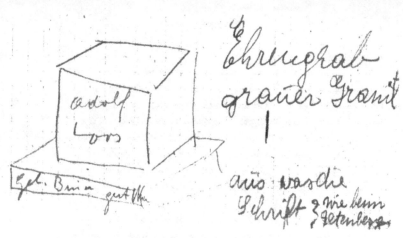

Drawing by Adolf Loos of his self-specified tombstone with "Born Brünn, Died Vienna" written below. As detailed on pages 83–84, this is the second drawing, as Claire's mirthful addition on the first version showing Loos being buried with all his wives was rejected by the architect.

In Claire's handwriting: "Honorary Grave grey granite." THE ALBERTINA MUSEUM, VIENNA

Envelope and letter to Claire Beck Loos from Josef Svatopluk Machar, Czechoslovak poet and essayist, on August 19, 1932, which was sent to Claire Beck Loos at her parents' apartment, Benešplatz 2, Pilsen, Czechoslovakia. Translation on pages 189–190.
PATERSON FAMILY ARCHIVE

Liebe Claire,

Ich habe soeben an Dich einen Brief expediert, in wele chem ich Dir auseinandersetzte, dass Deine Auffassung, bezüglich des Mannes den ich für Dich in Aussicht hatte ein Irrtum war, und dass ich diese Phrase lediglich zur Auskunft-Erteilung benötigte.

Nun, wollte es gerade der Zufall, dass ich heute, zu meinem Kinofreund ging und dort einen Herrn traf, der gerade diese Absichten hat, die ich in meinem vorigen Schreiben verneinen musste. Der Herr ist Franzose, ist genau im Alter Deines verst. Mannes, als Du Ihn heiratetest, ist Decorateur, und Archtekt, und sieht merkwürdigerweise sogar Deinem verst. Mann etwas ähnlich.

Ich bin der Ansicht, dass man diesem merkwürdigen Zufall nachgehen muss, undfalls Du Dich mit diesser Angelegenheit näher befassen willst, müsstest Du mir umgehend schreiben.

Wie Du mir geschrieben hast hast Du ursprünglich die Absicht gehabt, als Hausgehilfin nach England zu gehen. Ich würde Dir nun raten, dies unter allen Umständen anzustreben, denn dadurh bekommst Du die Einreise nach England, undgleichzeitig ein Transitvisum nach Frankreich. Bei dieser Gelegenheit, könntest Du mit diesem Herrn in Fühlung treten, und sehen, wass sich aus der Scahe machen lässt. Auf diese Weise wäre es für beide Teile vollkommen unverbindlich. Mir persönlich gefällt er sehr gut, und vor allem, würdest Du durch diese Heirat baldigst Französin.

Ich erwarte von Dir umgehend Nachricht, und bin mit den herzlichsten Grüssen,

Dein Schwager Stefan

To Claire Beck Loos from her brother-in-law, Stefan Schanzer, his copy of a letter he sent on April 7, 1939, after his escape to Paris. In the letter he suggests a possible solution to her emigration problem: marry an older man he met through his friend, a cinema owner in Paris. "The gentleman is French, is exactly the age of your husband [Loos] when you married him, is a designer and architect, and strangely enough, looks a little like your husband." Stefan agrees with Claire's plan to become a maid in England, in which case she could get a transit visa to come to Paris to meet this man, "that way it would be non-binding for both parties. [...] I personally like him very much, and above all, you would soon become French through this marriage." PATERSON FAMILY ARCHIVE

Einlieferungsschein Nr. 58 16

Klara Loos,

Prag VI., grüne game 4.

Prag, am 11. XII. 1941 HADEGA
Handelsgesellschaft b. H.

Aufbewahren!

Select Writings by Adolf Loos

Kindly reprinted with permission from
Jorun Johns and Karl Johns, publishers of
Ornament and Crime, selected essays
Edited by Adolf Opel
Translated by Mike Mitchell
© Ariadne Press 1998

POTTERY (1908)
[EXCERPT]

People of contemporary culture prefer their glass, china, majolica, and earthenware utensils to be undecorated. A drinking glass I want to use for drinking. Whether it be water, wine, beer, or spirits, the glass should be such that I enjoy the drink. That is the main thing. And for that reason I am happy to do without *olde worlde* mottoes or *art nouveau* decoration. There are, of course, ways of treating the glass so it shows off the color of the drink at its best. The same water may look stale and dull in one glass, and fresh as if straight from a mountain spring in another. That can be achieved through the quality of the material or the cutting. That is why, when buying glasses, one has a selection filled with water and chooses the best, with the result that those which are decorated so that they look as if green leeches are swimming around in them are left on the shelf.

But the glass should not only make the drink look good, it should also be good to drink out of. Glasses made during the last three centuries almost always fulfill both of these requirements. It was left to our age — no, I refuse to belittle our age: it was left to our artists to invent, besides unappetizing decoration, shapes that one cannot drink out of. There are tumblers from which the water runs out at the corners of your mouth on either side. There are liqueur glasses from which you can drink only half the liqueur. One should be very careful, then, with new shapes; it is generally better to stick to the old ones.

It is just the same with places. Our sensibilities are more delicate than during the Renaissance, when they would happily cut up their meat on mythological representations. Our sensibilities are also more delicate than during the Rococo, when people were unconcerned by the unappetizing greenish-gray color the onion pattern gave the soup. We prefer to eat off a white base. We do. The artists have a different opinion.

But the products of our potters are not used for cooking, eating, and drinking alone. Glass is used for windowpanes, ceramics for floor and wall tiles, for stoves and fireplaces, for flower vases and umbrella stands. And, finally, the artist can use clay, can shape it and glaze it and fire it, because he is inspired to portray people and animals, plants and stones, as he sees them.

Once I was in a coffeehouse with some applied artists. They were talking about setting up an experimental pottery station in the School of Applied Art. I was against everything the others suggested, and they were all against me. I was taking the view of the craftsman, the simple worker; they were taking the view of the artist.

Someone had brought along a marvelously red flower with velvety petals. It was in a glass on the table. One of them said, "See, Herr Loos, you just want people to make pots. But we want to try to create a glaze with the same color as this flower here." They were fired with enthusiasm for the idea. Yes, they would raid all the flowers in the world for new colors for their glazes. They talked and talked ...

Fortunately nature has given me one valuable gift: she made me hard of hearing. This enables me to sit among a noisy crowd of people arguing and debating, without having to listen to the rubbish they talk. I follow my own thoughts.

While they were talking, I thought of my own master potter. Not an artist. An artisan. He sees no flowers, he doesn't even like them, and he doesn't know their colors. But his soul is filled with colors which can be expressed only in clay and glaze.

I saw him in my mind's eye, sitting by his kiln, waiting. He has dreamed of colors the Creator forgot to dream up. No flower, no pearl, no ore has such colors. And now they are to become reality, are to sparkle and shine, to fill people with delight or sadness:

The fire is burning. Is it burning for me or against me?

Will it give tangible shape to my dreams, or will it eat them up? I know pottery traditions going back thousands of years; all the potters' tricks I know, I have used them all. But we have not yet reached the end. The spirit of the material has not yet been overcome.

May it never be! May the secrets of the material always remain mysteries to us. Otherwise my potter would not be sitting in happy torment at his kiln, waiting, hoping, dreaming of new colors and clays, which God in his wisdom forgot to create, in order to allow mankind to participate in the glorious joy of creation.

"So what have you to say about that, Herr Loos?" asked one of my companions. I said nothing.

Our artists sit at their drawing boards making designs for pottery. They are divided into two camps. One designs in all styles, the other only in the "modern" manner. Each camp has a thorough contempt for the other. But there is also a split in the modern camp. One side demands that ornament be taken from nature, the other that it come from imagination alone. But all three camps despise the simple master craftsman. Why? Because he is not a draftsman. But that is no harm to the potter. Tiles made ten years ago by Bigot in Paris have lost nothing of their charm, while designs the artists brought out five years ago bring on a migraine today, even in their creators. And that is true of all designs of this type.

Anyone who buys pottery should always bear that in mind. One does not spend one's money on something simply in order to be irritated by it three years later. Objects bearing the imprint of a creative craftsman's hand will always retain their value. Even if one likes them, one should reject objects with *art nouveau* decoration. We do not like them because they are beautiful, nor because they appeal to our sensibilities, but because people have tried to impose this style on us. One should rely on one's sensibilities, which one had before Hermann Bahr started writing about these things.

The drawing board and the kiln. A whole world separates them. On the one hand the precision of the compass, on the other the imprecision of chance, passion, dreams, and the mystery of creation.

IN PRAISE OF THE PRESENT (1908)
[EXCERPT]

When I look back over past centuries and ask myself in which age I would prefer to have lived, my answer is, in the present age. Oh, I know there were times when it was a joy to be alive. There were ages that had this or that advantage. And perhaps people in every other age have been happier than today. But in no age were people so beautifully, so practically, and so well dressed as today.

The idea that I had to drape a toga around myself first thing in the morning and had to keep that drapery hanging around me the whole day—the whole day, if you please!— in the same folds, would be enough to drive me to suicide. I want to walk, walk, walk, and then, if the fancy cakes me, jump onto a streetcar as it whizzes past. The Romans never walked. They stood around. And when I've had a bath and wrap the towel around me and tuck it in, in five minutes it's slipped to a quite different position. That's what my nerves are like.

The *cinquecento*, then? Fine. I'm to dress myself in silk and velvet so I look like an organ-grinder's monkey? No thanks.

Give me my own clothes any day. They are mankind's original dress. The materials are the same as Allfather

Woden wore for his cloak. The theatrical tailors dye it red or blue, but it was a Scottish plaid. Even in those days there were black sheep, and their wool, mixed with that of the white sheep, produced the first pepper-and-salt weave.

It is mankind's original dress. Who has not come across the great disappointment of travelers to distant continents when they realize they have been fooled as far as picturesque costumes are concerned. Ragamuffins by the Tigris and in Chicago, in China and in Cape Town are all dressed just the same as those in their home town. And a beggar in the days of Semiramis wore the same uniform as his present-day counterpart in Hicksburg.

It is mankind's original dress. A pauper in any age, and in any part of the world, could use our old trousers to cover his nakedness without introducing a foreign note to either the time or the landscape. It is not modern dress, it has always been with us, it has accompanied us down the centuries. The great lords of the past despised it, and went to the most stupid and unaesthetic lengths to avoid it. A ragamuffin has always been an aesthetic sight for the eye, a Louis XIV never.

At the end of the eighteenth and the beginning of the nineteenth centuries there lived in Vienna a man called Beethoven. The common people made fun of him. Short in stature, with a small head and his many little eccentricities, the middle classes objected to his compositions. What a pity, they said, there's something wrong with his ears. He thinks up the most horrible dissonances. However, he insists they are marvelous harmonies; therefore, since there is demonstrably nothing wrong with our ears, there must be something wrong with his.

The aristocracy, however, which recognized the duties it owed society stemming from the rights society had granted it, provided him with the money to have his works performed. The aristocracy also had the power to have an opera by Beethoven staged at the Imperial Opera. But the middle classes, who filled the seats in the theater, made the work such a flop that they could not risk a second performance.

A hundred years have passed since then, and today the middle classes are deeply moved by the works of the crazy, sick musician. Have they become aristocratic, are they like the nobles of 1814, struck with awe at the will of the genius? No, they have something wrong with their ears now, they all have Beethoven's ears. For a hundred years their ears have been abused by the dissonances of Saint Ludwig, and they have eventually been forced to give in to chem. All their anatomical details, all their ossicles, labyrinths, drums, and trumpets, have taken on the diseased forms of Beethoven's ears. And the funny face the urchins followed in the street, scoffing and jeering, has for the people come to represent the world of the spirit.

It is the spirit that shapes the body.

ORNAMENT AND EDUCATION (1924)
[EXCERPT]

Modern people, people with modern nerves, do not need ornament. On the contrary, they abhor it. All objects we call modern are without ornament. Since the French Revolution, our clothes, our machines, our leather goods, and all objects of everyday use have been without ornament. Apart, that is, from things belonging to women—but that is another story.

The only objects with ornamentation are those subject to one particular part of humanity—I call it the uncultured part—namely architects. Wherever practical objects are produced under the influence of architects, those objects are out of touch with the times, that is to say un-modern. That is of course also true of modern architects.

Individuals—and that therefore includes architects—are incapable of creating a new form. But architects keep on attempting the impossible, and keep on failing. Form and ornament are products of the subconscious collaboration of all members of a particular culture. Art is the complete opposite. Art is the product of the genius going his own way. His commission comes from God.

To waste art on objects of practical use demonstrates a lack of culture. Ornamentation means added labor. The sadism of the eighteenth century, burdening one's fellows with superfluous work, is alien to modern man. Even more alien is the ornamentation of primitive peoples, which is entirely religious or—symbolically—erotic in significance, and which, thanks to its primitive nature, comes close to art.

Lack of ornamentation does not mean lack of attractiveness, but is a new attraction and rouses the public from its lethargy. It is when the mill stops clacking that the miller wakes up.

SHORT HAIR: SHORT OR LONG— MASCULINE OR FEMININE? (1928)

Let us turn the question around and ask women what they think of men's short hair. They would probably answer that that is something that concerns men alone. In Zurich, the director of a hospital fired a nurse because she had her hair cut short. Would it be likely a woman director of a hospital would fire a male hospital orderly for the same reason? Men's hair can grow long—among the Germanic tribes it was gathered into a tail, in the Middle Ages it fell down over the shoulders, and during the renaissance it was cut short, following the ancient Roman custom. During the time of Louis XIV it came down over the shoulders again, was then braided into pigtails (I am still talking of men's hair), only, during and after the French Revolution, to be allowed to fall over the shoulders once more in long, free-flowing locks. Napolean had a Caesar cut, today we would call it a bob. Women also had their hair cut short—and why ever not?—and called the style the Titus look. Whether long hair is feminine and short hair masculine is something for the old women among the men to trouble their empty heads over. But to dictate to women that they must wear their hair long since long hair arouses men's desire and women's sole function is to stimulate this erotic excitement—no, that really is a piece of downright impudence! No woman would be so brazen as to make the secrets of her inner sex life into a moral commandment. In China, women wear trousers and men skirts; in the West, it is the other way around. But it is ridiculous to sound off about the divine order, nature, and morality in connection with such trifles. Working women—our female farm workers and dairymaids—wear trousers or short skirts. It is easy for women who have nothing to do to trail their clothes along behind them. But a man who presumes to dictate to women shows he regards women as sexual bondslaves. He would be better occupied seeing to his own dress. Women are perfectly capable of looking after theirs, thank you very much.

OSKAR KOKOSCHKA (1931)

I met Oskar Kokoschka in 1908. He had designed the poster for the Vienna Kunstschau exhibition. I had been told he was working for the Wiener Werkstätte and was employed in the German manner—art in the service of commerce—painting fans and drawing picture postcards. It was immediately clear to me that here one of the greatest crimes against the Holy Spirit was being committed. I sent for him. He came. What was he doing at the moment? Modeling a bust. (It was finished only inside his head.) Bought! What did it cost? A cigarette. Done! I never bargain, but in the end we agreed on fifty kronen.

For the Kunstschau he had drawn a life-size sketch for a tapestry. It was the high point of the show, and the Viennese poured in to laugh themselves silly. How I would have loved to purchase it, but it belonged to the Wiener Werksättte. It ended up with the exhibition refuse on the trash pile.

I promised him the same income if he left the Wiener Werkstätte and I looked for commissions for him. I sent him to see my wife, who was ill in Switzerland (Leysin), and asked Professor Forel, who lived in the vicinity, to get Kokoschka to do his portrait. Then I offered the picture to the directors of the museum in Berne for two hundred francs. Rejected. Then I submitted it for the exhibition in the Vienna Kunstlerhaus. Rejected. Then to the Klimt group for their exhibition in Rome. Rejected through the opposition to the Klimt group. It was only Mannheim that eventually had the courage to acquire it.

A picture costing two hundred kronen, and no collector, no gallery wanted to buy it.

When the building I designed on Michaelerplatz was being built, my enthusiasm for Kokoschka was taken as proof of my lack of ability.

And today?

Since I had asked almost the whole of Vienna to take over from me the task of supporting Kokoschka by buying a picture for a mere two hundred kronen, which they had scornfully rejected, their fury against me rose parallel to the rise in the price of Kokoschka's paintings.

Both the Viennese and I have survived it.

On the occasion of my sixtieth birthday Kokoschka sent me a letter that proves once again the greatest genius encompasses the greatest humanity.

ACKNOWLEDGMENTS

Tremendous thanks are due to the extended Beck family, who have preserved Claire Beck Loos' photographs and documents that accompany this book. Many of her letters as well as other photographs have been reprinted in *Escape Home: Rebuilding a Life After the Anschluss* by Claire's nephew Charles Paterson (né Karl Schanzer). Special thanks for this edition go to Janet Beck Wilson and Fonda Paterson. A longer version of these acknowledgments can be found in the hardcover version, *Adolf Loos — A Private Portrait* (DoppelHouse Press, 2011) along with further information about the family and an extended afterword.

The key to Claire's discreet shorthand for names of people has been reprinted from Adolf Opel's edition of *Adolf Loos Privat* (Böhlau, 1985). The portion of Otto Kapfinger's Afterword for *Adolf Loos Privat* (Czernin Verlag, 2007) appearing here was translated by Constance C. Pontasch, who also translated the excerpts from Karl Kraus' eulogy, Adolf Opel's *Adolf Loos — Der Mensch* (Prachner Verlag, 2002), and Alfred Polgar's defense of Adolf Loos in *Das Tagebuch*. Loos' letters to Claire were translated by Gunar Hochheiden from Burkhardt Rukschcio and Roland Schachel's *Adolf Loos — Leben und Werk*. The portion of Bořivoj Kriegerbeck's journal was translated by Ivan Margolius.

Maria Szadkowska at the Villa Müller kindly assured that two important photographs could be included here — that of Loos' sixtieth birthday party, which was held at the villa, and Claire's first known self-portrait.